Ask

Also by Daniel R. Solin

The Smartest Sales Book You'll Ever Read

The Smartest Money Book You'll Ever Read

The Smartest Portfolio You'll Ever Own

Timeless Investment Advice

The Smartest Retirement Book You'll Ever Read

The Smartest 401(k) Book You'll Ever Read

The Smartest Investment Book You'll Ever Read

Does Your Broker Owe You Money?

Ask

How to Relate to Anyone

Daniel R. Solin

New York Times Bestselling Author of
the *Smartest* Series of Books

Ask - Copyright © Daniel R. Solin, 2020

Silvercloud Publishing, LLC
Bonita Springs, FL 34134

Hardcover ISBN: 978-0-9748763-2-0
Mobi ISBN: 978-0-9748763-3-7

Library of Congress Control Number: 2020906248

Solin,Daniel R.
Ask/Daniel R. Solin
Issued also as ePub, ePDF and mobiebooks.
Includes bibliographical references and index.

Cover design: James Jones Book Design - jamesjonesbookdesign@gmail.com
Interior layout: Tracy Atkins - atkins.tracy@gmail.com

Printed in the United States of America
Publisher's Cataloging-in-Publication data
First Edition

For permission requests, quantity sales, branding opportunities, strategic alliances, partnerships, media inquiries, speaking engagements, and orders by U.S. trade bookstores and wholesalers, please contact:

Dan Solin
dansolin@ebadvisormarketing.com
(239) 949-1606.

To those of you who attended my sessions and provided feedback, you were the inspiration for this book.

My Thanks

It takes a village to write a book. I benefited greatly from the wisdom of some wonderful people. I could not have written this book without them.

I had the pleasure of working with D. Olson Pook, an extraordinary developmental editor. He worked tirelessly (and patiently) to refine my initial concept and sharpen my thinking.

My wife, Patricia A. Solin, is a wonderful artist and excellent editor. She has journeyed with me through this book, my previous books, and my life. With every draft, her edits honed the message, kept me on track, intensified my focus, and made the final manuscript as relatable as possible.

I also benefited from the excellent comments of my daughter-in-law, Mandy Solin, my friend, Joel McFarland, MD, my consulting neuroscientist, Jocelyne Whitehead, Joy Xiang, who formatted the endnotes, Mary H. Eagan, my proofreader, and my author's assistant, Danielle Acee.

In the end, the responsibility for any errors is mine alone.

Contents

Preface

Ask is a journey we will take together.

Have you ever wondered why a meeting went so badly? Or why you have such trouble developing a meaningful relationship with certain people in your business and personal life? Or why you aren't more successful?

I've spent years researching those issues, motivated by my own experiences. Here's what I found.

It's not about us. It's not about trying to be witty, charming or entertaining. It's not about conveying information or demonstrating expertise. It's about listening to others and asking them questions.

I used to believe what I was saying was more important than what I was hearing. Instead of really listening, I was just waiting for the other person to stop talking. I had an agenda and was eager to convey it.

As a consequence, my interactions with others were like two billiard balls bouncing off each other. Making contact sometimes just drove the other person further away.

Do you ever have a similar feeling?

Then I did some research. What I found was stunning.

When we empower others to talk about themselves, the brain activity in those people is similar to when they're engaged in their most pleasurable activities. Talking about yourself releases certain hormones that make you feel good. Doing so causes you to project traits of likeability and trustworthiness onto the person who encourages you to talk.

Conversely, trying to persuade someone about anything releases cortisol, the stress hormone. Even worse, talking non-stop about anything for more than just a few minutes can make the other person feel diminished and trivialized. It can even cause them to experience the same hormonal response as when they are in physical pain.

Could improving relationships be as simple as talking less while empowering the other person to talk more? Could focusing on others in a genuine and sincere way, and getting them to talk about themselves, be the key? And if that's true, just how difficult is it for us to sublimate our egos, abandon our agenda, and implement these basic principles?

Compelling research is great, but can it be implemented in the real world?

I've spent the past four years speaking about my findings to thousands of people all over the world. Initially, my audience was composed of investment advisors. They reported a massive increase (over $1 billion in new assets under management) by using the basic principles discussed in this book. I then branched out and started speaking to those engaged in other businesses. Their response was similar.

Ask had a surprising collateral benefit. Many who implemented my findings told me their personal relationships with friends, family, and especially their children, were transformed.

Here's one particularly poignant example. After one of my talks, a member of the audience approached me and said he was about to go to lunch with his son. They had been estranged because the father wanted the son to become an investment advisor, and the son wanted to pursue a career as a musician. He asked if these principles would be effective in the context of the lunch. I told him I was confident he could change his relationship with his son by just asking thoughtful questions and putting aside his own agenda.

Later, he wrote me a touching e-mail, telling me the lunch went "great." All he did was ask his son questions about his music. He listened carefully to the responses, and then asked follow-up questions. His son spoke for almost all the time they were together. The father refrained from offering any advice.

At the end of the lunch, they embraced, and both were teary-eyed (as was I when I read his e-mail). They may never agree on the right career path, but they have newfound respect for each other.

I've received this type of positive feedback hundreds of times.

In my own life, implementing my findings has increased my level of personal happiness and deepened my relationships. People project the nicest qualities onto me, like kindness, thoughtfulness and insight, whenever I encourage them to talk about themselves.

The next logical step in my journey was to share that research with everyone. So I began to write *Ask*.

If you're interested in reading the underlying studies, you can find them in the Endnotes. If you're reading the e-book version, you can click on the links for more details.

Before you turn the page to start learning about *Ask*, I want to share one caveat: what you'll find in *Ask* won't solve all your relationship issues. But implementing *Ask* will immediately transform those relationships you want to improve, and make every day of your life (and the lives of those with whom you interact) happier and more positive.

At the end of this journey, you really will be able to relate to anyone.

Introduction

Ask is easy to understand and intuitively obvious, but it takes some effort to implement. At a reception for a recent event where I spoke to an audience about how they could use *Ask*, I was reminded how difficult this could be.

A young woman approached and introduced herself. She was an investment advisor based on the West Coast. I asked her to tell me about herself and how she had decided to pursue a career in finance, a historically male-dominated profession.

She answered briefly, and then said, "Dan, I want to write a book. Can you tell me how you got started, and what that journey has been like for you?" I was flattered by the question. Before I realized it, I began a long soliloquy in which I gave her far more information than she probably wanted.

I fell into the trap I just spent over an hour telling others to avoid. Mercifully, I realized what was happening, and quickly pivoted to ask her to tell me more about the book she wanted to write.

The balance of our conversation proceeded with her talking about a subject close to her heart, and with me asking more questions.

Here's what struck me from this encounter: I teach the importance of asking questions, but I'm not immune to the pleasure we all derive from talking about ourselves. Staying focused on the other person is a critical part of *Ask*.

That incident brought home how challenging focusing intently on others can be. It reinforced my conviction that everyone might benefit if I summarized my research in an easy-to-use way.

Here's how we can take this journey together.

In Part One, we'll identify an elusive but achievable goal – becoming happier. We'll uncover some strategies that work and others to avoid. Some findings are surprising; others are counterintuitive.

Did you know you might be happier and more successful with *low* self-confidence? Or that positive thinking may make it *less* likely we'll reach our goals? Research has conclusively shown there's one surprising factor in our lives that's a predictor for both happiness and health. We'll explore what it is and how to nurture it.

In Part Two, we'll discuss traits most of us need to improve in order to implement *Ask* successfully. For example, few of us realize how essential self-awareness is to improving our relationships. We can better understand its importance through the lens of the differences between introverts and extroverts.

In Part Three, we'll explore the neuroscience and psychology research underlying *Ask,* and show how to use those findings to improve your interactions in every context.

Ever wonder why it can feel so counter-productive to explain your point of view or offer advice? Or why it's so difficult to persuade others that our point of view is "right"?

In Part Four, we'll focus on the compelling role emotions play in relationships. We'll harness this knowledge to deepen your relationships.

In Part Five, we'll look at the kind of roadblocks that routinely crop up when implementing *Ask*, and offer suggestions for dealing with them. We'll also explore difficult situations where you can apply *Ask* to ease tension and generate immediate goodwill.

Let's get started. A big change is about to happen.

•Part One•

Why Ask?

How much of your happiness
is within your control?

If you want others to be happy, practice compassion.
If you want to be happy, practice compassion.
−Dalai Lama

Chapter One

What Really Makes Us Happy?

W hen it comes to happiness, about the only thing researchers agree on is that it's a worthy goal. There's disagreement about what it is, how to achieve it, and even how much happiness is enough. Behind the philosophical questions, there's an even more pragmatic one: How much control do we have over our happiness?

This question has been exhaustively studied, and the findings are quite revealing. The advice offered in *Ask* is modeled on this research.

Good news

In her book, *The How of Happiness: A Scientific Approach to Getting the Life You Want*, Sonja Lyubomirsky concluded that 50% of the *variance* in happiness is determined by our genes, and an additional 10% is determined by circumstances, leaving 40% within our control. The 50% number emerged out of studies of twins, as well as of lottery winners and paraplegics, which revealed that humans have natural "starting points" for their happiness.

The researchers found recent accident victims reported more happiness from everyday pleasures (chatting with a friend, watching television, laughing at a joke) than lottery winners, although the differences were small. The authors of the study noted that "the paraplegic rating of present happiness is still above the midpoint of the scale and ... the accident victims did not appear nearly as unhappy as might have been expected."

Even in dire circumstances, we retain the ability to control a meaningful portion of our level of happiness.

Importantly, research also uncovered that only 10% of the variance in happiness is determined by our circumstances.

David Schkade and Daniel Kahneman found that while many people believe that changing external circumstances (like moving to California or buying a new car) might make them happier, over time the impact is statistically insignificant.

This 50/10/40 formula is often misinterpreted as demonstrating that we have the ability to control 40% of our level of happiness. But that's not what Lyubomirsky discovered. Her percentages explain why there is a *difference* in happiness levels between different people.

If my happiness level is a 10 out of 10 and yours is an 8, half of that two-point difference might be attributable to genetics, but almost the same amount is attributable to factors you can control. While a 10 might be out of reach, 9 is certainly within your grasp.

So how do we harness the remaining 40% of the happiness variance that is within our control? We can shape our happiness through intentional activity on our part, whether it's behavioral (exercise), cognitive ("counting one's blessings"), or volitional (striving for a goal).

Happiness researchers note that while circumstances (like being married) don't make you happy, your actions in those circumstances do: a husband can buy his wife flowers (behavioral), appreciate her positive qualities (cognitive), and even engage in her favorite pursuits (volitional).

Todd Kashdan, professor of psychology at George Mason University, observes that environmental factors can "switch genes on and off," affecting our happiness. Although genetics might have played a meaningful role earlier in our lives, as we age, our life experiences have far more influence on our thoughts, feelings, and behavior. Because we're older, we're also more skilled at pursuing activities that bring us happiness. The takeaway is our happiness is malleable and partially within our control.

One researcher aptly summed up the situation by concluding that "happiness is not a hard science" in the way the universe is subject to the laws of physics. Instead of applying an overly simplistic formula for how much happiness we control, let's focus instead on how to have a positive impact on it.

Happiness hacks

I like to divide my life into two buckets – things I can control and things I can't. I try to focus on the former and spend as little time as possible on the latter. Researchers recommend this strategy. But they have some important insights into *how* best to implement activities that you find improve your happiness:

- Make them *episodic*. Habitual non-varying activities don't improve your happiness. Researchers say you should only perform meaningful activities that keep you feeling fresh and make you feel good. The same exercise routine at the same time of day might be convenient, but over time it will not make you as happy as switching your walking route or varying the time of day you go for a run.

- Make them *varied*. This reduces the likelihood of an activity becoming routine to the point of becoming a "habit treadmill," and keep it pointed towards genuine happiness. Runners might try switching things up and go for a hike or swim; walkers should add lifting weights or stretching to the mix.

- Make them *fit*. Activities that bring you happiness match your interests and skill levels so you can perform them and find them intrinsically rewarding. Activities that are our "signature strengths" often bring us happiness, whether it's knitting, woodworking, or even just reading. But the match can go beyond just the type of activity. Later, I'll talk about the research into introverts and extroverts, but for now it's worth noting that extroverted knitters find even more happiness in a knitting circle, but introverts might find their happiness sapped if they were forced to join a group.

- Make an *effort*. Researchers stress you must make an effort to be happy – not just initiating the activity, but carrying it out and maintaining it over time. Make it both self-reinforcing and self-sustaining. Find the time to pick up the knitting needles, schedule a date to meet with other knitters, and complete the sweater you are making. Goal completion is important. Once you put the final touches on, you're more likely to seek out the next challenge that leads to even more happiness.

Take charge of your happiness and make increasing it a priority. Everything within *Ask* is within your control, fits within these recommendations, and involves daily activities that play a critical role in improving your happiness level.

Health hacks

If you're in poor health, it's difficult to take steps to become happier.

Unfortunately, some aspects of our health are beyond our control, like a genetically inherited condition, access to quality health care, and adverse environmental conditions. On the flip side, there are many choices we can make that positively impact our health. In John Medina's *Brain Rules*, he argues that one of the greatest predictors of achieving happiness and aging successfully is whether or not you live a sedentary lifestyle.

The difference between pushing a walker while staring vacantly ahead in a nursing home, and thriving physically and mentally as you age is directly related to exercise. Seniors who exercised outperformed couch potatoes in cognitive tests measuring long-term memory, reasoning, attention, problem-solving skill, and "fluid intelligence tasks" (which test the ability to reason quickly and improvise). You'll need a clear head to form goals and act on them. And what's true for seniors is true at every age.

Some people are deterred from exercising because they believe only very strenuous exercise is beneficial. Not true.

Moderate exercise is better than no movement at all. Just walking several times a week benefits the brain. The "gold standard" is aerobic exercise for 30 minutes, two to three times a week. If you increase that recommendation to a 20-minute walk each day, your risk of a stroke decreases by over 50%, and the danger of developing heart disease and diabetes is also greatly reduced.

The benefits aren't just physical. Exercise has been shown to be successful in treating depression and anxiety. Aerobic activity just twice a week halves your risk of general dementia and cuts your risk of Alzheimer's by 60%. Add in weight training, and you'll get even more cognitive benefits. In Medina's words, "Physical activity is cognitive candy."

Can we eat our way to happiness?

You have no doubt heard so much about the relationship between diet and health that you've become numb to it. Here's a fact from the Center for Science in the Public Interest that may surprise you: an unhealthy diet contributes to approximately 678,000 deaths each year in the U.S.

Did you know sugar is as bad for you as cigarettes and that you may be consuming 46 hidden teaspoons of sugar a day? Or that eating more fruit can improve your liver health? Or that 90 percent of Americans consume too much sodium, which raises blood pressure and contributes to heart disease?

The irony is that it's relatively simple to understand what constitutes a healthy diet. Reduce calories, saturated fat, sodium, and added sugars. Increase fruits, vegetables, whole grains, calcium and fiber.

Changing our exercise and eating habits can be challenging. But it's a no-brainer measured against the cost of not doing so.

Helping yourself by helping others

Being kind and compassionate is a quick and easy path to increased happiness.

The Dalai Lama observed that "when we feel love and kindness toward others, it not only makes others feel loved and cared for, but it helps us also to develop inner happiness and peace."

You don't need to be the Dalai Lama to practice compassion and reap the benefits. Opportunities abound: stopping a car to help an elderly woman navigate a busy street safely; giving a compliment to a colleague or friend; or sending a note expressing gratitude to someone who impacted your life in a positive way.

The feelings of satisfaction and happiness felt by those engaged in kind and caring behavior are supported by many studies. There's compelling research that "love and caring expressed in doing good for others lead people to have healthier, happier lives." Kindness has been shown to reduce depression, promote better physical health, and increase positive feelings we have about ourselves.

One study from the United Kingdom found communities where more people volunteered had "less crime, better schools, and happier, healthier residents." The researchers observed a link "between helping others and enjoying a good quality of life." In short, the kind of mindfulness required to be compassionate is a net gain. It reduces stress and prepares us to be happy. Our brains actually find it more pleasurable to be compassionate than to be selfish.

Disconnect to be happier

Here's a shocking statistic: one-third of respondents in a study said they would rather give up sex for a week (or even brushing their teeth) than go without their mobile devices. Most people check their smartphones every 12 minutes, or on average, eighty times a day.

Our compulsion to stay connected and push the limits of what we can accomplish materially impacts our energy levels. It's stressing us out and detracting from our happiness.

Sleep is another area we can examine. What's the trade-off between sleep and being more productive?

There's evidence that sleeping more boosts energy levels and productivity. That seems counterintuitive, yet it was the finding of a study that looked at the sleep habits of eleven healthy students on the Stanford University men's varsity basketball team. Increasing the number of hours the participants slept to ten hours a night significantly improved their free-throw percentages and overall accuracy. Other studies found a positive impact of naps on the performance of air traffic controllers.

It's not just athletes and individuals in high-stakes jobs who benefit from more rest and less stress. Employees from all industries who take more vacations are more productive. Those who take at least eleven of their vacation days are more likely to receive a bonus or raise. According to the *Harvard Business Review*, "taking more vacations results in greater success at work as well as lower stress and more happiness at work and home."

Vacations are great, but what can you do for the other fifty weeks of the year? There's actually a growing body of research that points to the positive impact of meditation.

Meditation has been discussed in hundreds of research studies. Its benefits include increased empathy, less stress, greater self-awareness, and better mental and physical health. Meditation can also increase your creativity and reduce pain levels. Those who meditate experience more calm and higher levels of happiness than those who don't.

A number of apps are available to get you started. Some of the better-known ones are The Mindfulness App, Headspace, Calm, 10% Happier and Breathe.

The grateful head

When I asked a friend how he was doing, here's what he said: "Every day I sit down for my morning coffee and contemplate my day, and I'm grateful."

He's on to something. The practice of gratitude can make a powerful contribution to your happiness.

The benefits of gratitude are well-researched. One study found being consciously grateful maximized the participants' level of contentment. Those who expressed gratitude were also more physically fit and had fewer health issues than those who didn't. Other long-lasting benefits of gratitude include improved relationships and an overall increase in happiness.

One of the most vivid examples of the impact of showing gratitude is found in a video from SoulPancake. Participants were asked to call someone who made a positive contribution in their life and express their gratitude. Those who did increased their level of happiness (from the beginning to the end of the experiment) as much as twenty percent. The biggest increase in happiness came from the person who was the *least* happy initially.

It's easy to start the practice of gratitude. Keep track of all the positive things in your life. Even better, express those feelings to family and friends. Take the time to write a note to acknowledge the importance of someone in your life. It can have an outsized impact on your level of happiness – and theirs.

All of these elements contribute to our happiness, but we haven't yet touched on the most important one.

What's more important than genetics?

Happiness involves a lot of different ingredients, but one factor plays a paramount role. According to a Harvard study that has been ongoing for almost eighty years, nothing is more important than healthy, meaningful relationships. Nurturing relationships makes us happier *and* healthier. This connection is so powerful that having solid relationships at age fifty was a better predictor of physical health thirty years later than cholesterol levels.

The study also found those with high marital satisfaction had better mental health, were less depressed, and had better cognitive ability. One of the researchers summed up the findings in stark terms: "...the key to healthy aging is relationships, relationships, relationships." The researchers found the role of genetics was *less* important than the level of satisfaction with relationships in midlife.

Healthy relationships also correlate with less stress, quicker healing, smarter lifestyle choices, and having a greater sense of purpose. Good relationships are plainly the key to a longer, happier life.

While the goal of having positive relationships is crucial, most of the studies never discuss this critical issue: *How* do you do it?

Fortunately, there's solid research in the fields of psychology and neuroscience that provide a science-based roadmap to improved relationships. What really struck me was how easily the research could be understood and implemented.

I took the disparate studies and identified the underlying actions that were scientifically proven to have a positive impact on *all* interactions. *Ask* is the result.

What's the Point?

We have meaningful control over our happiness.

For every complex problem, there's a solution
that is simple, neat, and wrong.
−H.L. Mencken

Chapter Two

Self Help or Self Harm?

If you want to transform your relationships it's important to look beyond simplistic advice. *Ask* is based on science, not unsupported musings.

Too good to be true?

Steven Novella, an academic clinical neurologist at the Yale University School of Medicine, observed that "the big sellers in the self-help industry seem to be completely disconnected" from published evidence. According to Dr. Novella, "What they are selling are made-up easy answers, personality, and gimmicks."

The "common hook" of these books, he notes, is the flawed view that you can materially improve your life just by *thinking* about better outcomes. Much of the advice is demonstrably wrong, but the message and messengers have a certain appeal – if you are looking for easy solutions to complex problems.

Intuitively, we all know that just reading about improving our lives and increasing our happiness probably won't result in genuine change. As one commentator noted, "In order to succeed or improve in any area of your life, you need to actually do something."

Author and blogger Mark Manson believes many self-help books reinforce perceptions of inferiority and shame, encourage avoidance of the underlying issue, and create unrealistic expectations. The advice they offer typically isn't scientifically validated, and worst of all, they foster "the perception of progress and not progress itself."

Ask is premised on sound, peer-reviewed research. It doesn't offer quick fixes or set unrealistic expectations.

Simple...and wrong

We all seek simple solutions to complex issues. Heuristics help explain the appeal of easy solutions.

Heuristics are mental shortcuts that permit us to make quick and efficient judgments. We're confronted daily with a mountain of data. We often don't have the time -- or want to make the effort -- to crunch that data and make a rational, evidence-based decision. That's why we resort to shortcuts.

Heuristics aren't always bad. Some decisions don't merit a comprehensive analysis, like which movie you should see. Heuristics are more problematic when they lead to poor decisions based on inadequate information.

When we employ heuristics to categorize an entire group of people, they may lead us to hold prejudicial and discriminatory views.

Not all truck drivers are short, fat, and male. Not all professors are tall, bearded, and wear jackets with elbow patches. We've come a long way in changing our language to counter previously common, built-in stereotypes. Think about past images associated with words like "stewardess." "Flight attendant" better reflects the reality of that role today. Few of us are surprised to discover that most professions are well-represented by both genders.

Many people will engage in heuristics rather than take the time to really think through complex issues. That's the appeal of many "solutions" commonly offered in self-help books.

Is seeing believing?

Some self-help books extol the benefit of "visualizing" your goal. You've probably heard this advice. It tells you to "see" the results you want to achieve, often accompanied by an appealing motivational phrase like, "If you can dream it, you can achieve it." There's little scientific support for the notion that simply visualizing a goal makes it more likely you will achieve it.

There's a critical difference between visualizing results and visualizing the *actions* it will take to achieve those results. Nothing illustrates this issue better than a well-publicized debacle that occurred in July, 2012. The event – called "Unleash the Power Within" – was sponsored by famous motivational speaker Anthony Robbins. Twenty-one people were treated for second and third-degree burns caused when they were encouraged to walk barefoot over hot coals.

While the injury to their feet was painful, it paled in comparison to the damage to their pride and self-esteem. One participant attributed his failure to not being at his "peak state," and others blamed themselves for getting burned.

The problem for those who got burned wasn't their inability to "think positively." It was their misplaced reliance on visualizing their goals, which they naively believed could defeat the laws of physics.

In order to implement meaningful changes in your life, you need to focus on what's within your power to influence and stop blaming yourself for things over which you have little or no control.

Don't dream it, be it

There's a legitimate role for positive thinking when it's based on reality. It's realistic to believe hard work is often correlated with career advancement. It's a fantasy to believe buying a lottery ticket is likely to make you wealthy beyond your wildest dreams.

Studies indicate positive *expectations*, realistically based on past experience, are predictive of future results. Positive *fantasies* are predictive of low effort and sub-optimal results. As psychologist Jeremy Dean noted, "...expectations are built on solid foundations while positive fantasies are often built on thin air."

Be skeptical of advice that encourages positive fantasy. Émile Coué, a French psychologist and pharmacist in the early twentieth century, recommended repeating, "Every day, in every way, I'm getting better and better." Repeating that mantra might make you feel good, but it won't actually make you "better and better."

Lose confidence in self-confidence

There's nothing in *Ask* about boosting your self-confidence – and for a good reason.

There's considerable evidence having *low* self-confidence makes you more aware of your shortcomings. The ability to be self-critical can propel you to achieve success. Those who brim with self-confidence tend to ignore negative feedback and can come across as arrogant. They are also less likely to accept responsibility for errors, and more likely to blame others for mistakes.

Low (but not too low) self-confidence can make you work harder to achieve your goals. You're more motivated to put in the time and effort to improve.

Be kind to yourself

This quote from motivational author Louise Hay is one of my favorites: *Remember, you have been criticizing yourself for years and it hasn't worked. Try approving of yourself and see what happens.*

I vividly remember an incident that occurred after I gave a talk to over 400 investors. I asked the sponsor to send me the feedback elicited from the audience without filtering it. The feedback was overwhelmingly positive, with one glaring exception. One person didn't like the message or the messenger. He expressed his views in very personal terms. Despite the overwhelmingly positive feedback, that one comment haunted me.

I was experiencing a lack of self-compassion. As a psychiatrist once told a friend, "A 90 is still an A." Hoping that 100 percent of my audience would be captivated by my message was unrealistic. Of course, I wanted to evaluate what caused the negative reaction and what I could have done differently. But my reaction should also have been to engage in more self-compassion.

The Center for Mindful Self-Compassion offers a helpful perspective on the issue: "Self-compassion involves responding in the same supportive and understanding way you would with a good friend when you yourself encounter difficulties, fall short of a goal, or notice something you don't like about yourself."

If a friend recounted an experience similar to mine, how would I react?

I would tell her what a great job she did as indicated by the overwhelmingly positive feedback. I would be supportive rather than negative and critical. Why should I be more compassionate with her than I am with myself?

There's evidence those who are more forgiving and nurturing toward themselves are healthier, have better relationships, and have a better self-image. They also have lower levels of anxiety and depression.

We tend to be too harsh when judging ourselves. Taking care of our mind and body, and being more self-supportive, can go a long way toward increasing our happiness.

Small molecules. Big impact

There's exciting research that explains the role oxytocin and dopamine play in achieving a higher level of happiness. These are two of the most powerful molecules your brain produces. They provide the neurochemical basis for what underlies *Ask*.

The human brain is a crowded place, home to hundreds of billions of cells, with trillions of molecules being shuffled between them. A molecule is a group of atoms organized into a particular design. Two types of molecules play a central role in the brain's operation: hormones and neurotransmitters.

Hormones are molecules produced by special structures in the brain and other parts of the body that enter the bloodstream and exert their effects on different organs and tissues – including the brain. Neurotransmitters are molecules that transmit messages between brain cells, giving rise to our thoughts and emotions.

One of the most mysterious yet influential hormones on human interaction is oxytocin. It's produced deep within the brain, in a structure known as the hypothalamus, before being secreted into the bloodstream. It's then carried to target cells around the brain and body where it exerts its effects.

While science has yet to unlock all of oxytocin's secrets, there's a lot about it we do know. Oxytocin is a rare breed of hormone. In the brain, oxytocin levels are increased during sexual arousal, trust, and mother-infant bonding. That's why oxytocin has been called the "love hormone" and the "cuddle chemical."

It got this reputation from a series of studies that appeared to demonstrate that sniffing oxytocin (and thereby increasing its presence in the bloodstream) "makes people more generous, cooperative, empathetic and constructive", These findings led to the conclusion that the release of oxytocin causes us to trust others, thereby adding the name, "the moral molecule," to its attributes. Some have questioned the validity of these studies, describing the science underlying them as "weak".

A number of additional studies have led researchers to conclude that oxytocin release leads to "an emotional sense of safety," as well as "the capacity to be close to and sensitive to others" – both critical parts of forming relationships with others.

Dopamine is another powerful molecule. It acts as a neurotransmitter in our brains. Dopamine motivates us to achieve our goals and rewards us with a feeling of satisfaction. Levels of dopamine increase when the brain recognizes reward or pleasure. When we feel really good (eating our favorite foods, engaging in sex), our dopamine levels increase as well.

Both oxytocin and dopamine make us feel good. They are critical components in the complex neurochemical balancing act within our brain. They are intimately connected with actions that are the focus of this book.

Ask focuses on showing you how to increase the levels of these molecules *in others*, so they'll feel great about themselves...and you. Ignoring the neurochemical state of the person you're trying to build a better relationship with is like trying to tango without a partner.

That's the essence of *Ask* and the reason it's so effective.

What's the Point?

Ask is based on solid, peer-reviewed research in the fields of psychology and neuroscience.

When we fear what other people think about us,
we are frequently more focused on 'being interesting'
and less focused on 'taking an interest.'
–John Yokoyama

Chapter Three

Ever Try to Engage a Goldfish?

I mproving a relationship by engaging the other person can dramatically affect their happiness as well as our own. This Chapter provides insight about how to engage people by changing their brain chemistry.

Engagement offers both immediate and long-lasting rewards. Creating it leads to better relationships, deeper understanding, and more self-satisfaction.

There's no shortage of advice about engagement. Your local bookstore is brimming with books offering all sorts of solutions, from quick fixes to years-long programs. These books often promise to help you deepen your focus and increase your attention span, making you more conscious and alert to your surroundings.

Unfortunately, much of the advice offered is unsupported – and even contradicted – by peer-reviewed evidence. It doesn't get to the core of happiness in relationships – the need to engage *others*.

A new twist on "engagement"

Let's first agree on what's meant by "engagement." When I ask audiences for a definition, I usually get an answer that centers on the idea that *the other person is totally interested in what I'm saying.*

There's a fundamental flaw in this view. The problem is that it's you who's engaged, and not your listener. You are commanding the floor, and you are directing the flow of the conversation. No wonder you're engaged. But your listener? Rather than nodding in assent, they might just be nodding off.

If your goal is to achieve a higher level of engagement in your relationships, flip this idea on its head. If you want to engage with someone, you'll need to step back, stop talking, and listen.

What is it about our lives that makes us believe talking instead of listening leads to engagement? We now talk more – through emails, texts, and social media – than ever before. We will send close to 300 million emails this year and almost twice as many texts. That's a lot of time talking. No wonder we think talking is engaging.

All that talking makes it difficult for us to engage. British researchers have shown that our ability to engage someone is negatively affected by the mere presence of our cell phones. They created an ingenious experiment where they asked pairs of strangers to sit down and engage in conversation. In half the rooms, they placed a cell phone on the table, and in the other half, there was no technology present.

After the conversations were over, they asked participants to rate the quality of the relationship they had established. Remember, the cell phone wasn't even on, and no one placed a call or was sent a text during the experiment. The phone didn't even belong to either person. It was as inanimate and unresponsive an object as if it were a banana. Still, participants in the cell phone rooms reported the quality of their relationship suffered in comparison to those in a room without a cell phone.

Their level of engagement was negatively impacted because a silent, unused phone posed such a distraction.

Minds wander

The presence of the phone points to a second issue. Humans have evolved to be wired with very short attention spans. Studies show both students and professionals will "mentally check out" of a lecture after only ten minutes, with retention levels plummeting at that point.

It's no different in relationships. Daniel Goleman's extensive research into the brain demonstrated that our minds tend to wander about 50 percent of the time, no matter what the activity (with the exception of sex).

The problem is twofold. Talking doesn't lead to engagement. Even if it did, a passive listener wouldn't focus long enough to retain what we have to say.

We're not at a loss to explain why talkers are fully engaged, but listeners are not. The explanation goes to the heart of why you can speed up the playback of a podcast or audiobook, yet still understand everything the speaker is saying.

When you talk, your brain doesn't have the capacity to focus on anything other than what you are saying (or what you are about to say). That's because, despite all the hype about multitasking, our brains in reality function serially.

While the average person speaks between 100 to125 words a minute, the brain of a listener can process at the rate of 400 words a minute. Think about that for a moment. A speaker might be wholly engaged while talking at 100 words a minute, but 75 percent of the processing capacity of the listener is free to wander – which is precisely what happens.

Great presenters. Bored audiences

I once had the experience of speaking at a conference right after a very charismatic speaker. With every dramatic and expansive gesture, my heart sank. His delivery was compelling. His PowerPoint slides were beautifully designed. His subject matter was interesting. All I could think was how I could never be that good.

After about ten minutes, I noticed something interesting: the audience began to fidget. Some people were checking their smartphones; others got up to get coffee or use the restrooms.

Nothing about his delivery had changed. He was still one of the most compelling speakers I'd ever heard. But when I did the research into the attention span of audiences, I found the answer to why this most compelling of speakers could not command his audience's full attention. They needed something else to do.

Here's the bottom line: the brain doesn't like listening, even for a short time. How short? It turns out we massively underestimate our attention spans. According to a study by Microsoft, we start to lose our ability to concentrate after *eight seconds*. The average attention span for a goldfish is one second longer.

This changes everything

So the stage is set. Just talking to an audience (whether to one or one thousand people) won't hold their attention for very long (even though *you* are fully engaged). We also know that passively listening (even to the most compelling speaker) won't prevent your mind from wandering.

Despite these obstacles, there is a way to engage anyone, at any time, on any subject and in any context.

You can achieve this result with a room full of people, or with just a single person sitting across from you. The engagement will be total, and the person or persons you're engaging will be focused on *the topic of your choosing* to the exclusion of everything else. They will be completely engaged.

I suspect you're thinking there must be a gimmick. There isn't. You can get these results without any tricks.

Here's how you do it: Ask your audience a question.

Ask a real and engaging question that captures their interest. Ask a question that shows you care about their perspective and you're listening to them. Ask a question and then have them answer it – *really* answer it. Then ask follow-up questions that show you are actually listening.

Do this and your audience's engagement will be total.

A great opening

Terry Gross is an expert interviewer. She's the host of NPR's popular *Fresh Air* program, where she has questioned thousands of people for over 40 years. In an article by Jolie Kerr in the *New York Times*, Gross divulged her interview secrets.

Gross recommends starting a conversation by asking, "Tell me about yourself." Not, "Tell me about your day," or even, "How are you today?" Instead, you ask a question that goes to the core of the person. Her goal is to find out how the interviewee became who they are.

Journalists often use open-ended questions that begin with *why* or *how*. That's because it's their job to elicit a good story. Why is it we so rarely view conversation as a chance to gently interview the other person? Is it because we're too busy talking ourselves?

If someone approached you and sincerely asked you to tell them about yourself, and then followed up in a way that showed that they had been paying close attention to what you'd just said, how engaged would you be?

That's the power of the right question.

I can't hear you

Asking the right question is only half of the equation. It needs to be followed by active, intentional listening. This has been the topic of considerable research for the past sixty years, and yet very little of it has filtered into the popular consciousness in ways that affect how we listen. Are you truly *listening* when you give a friend's social media post a "like"? The research says you're not.

You might ask yourself whether implementing *Ask* is even possible. If talking about yourself is so powerful, can you actually stop talking and actively listen?

It's a fair question. Researchers have shown that if you put a price on different conversational topics, people are willing to be paid considerably less if they are allowed to talk about themselves. What's to stop you from interrupting a person's response to add your own two cents?

This is what happens every day in conversations with our loved ones and others. We interrupt, cut off, or talk over the other person in order to establish our agenda or interpretation of the facts.

The good news is that active listening can be taught. Researchers in Australia have shown that when we tune in not just to the words that are being said, but also to the way those words are delivered through facial expressions and body language, we can keep our attention fully focused on the person speaking.

There are a host of reasons why you should actively listen, from sheer politeness to situations where it's critical in order to do your job. The single most important reason is the most obvious and yet the least practiced: to be able to ask a thoughtful follow-up question.

Follow-up or move on

Imagine someone approached you and asked a thoughtful question. You answer it and it looks like they are listening closely. But when your questioner next speaks, they change the subject. Were they really listening?

That's why asking a single question is not enough. If you want to engage your audience, you have to actively listen, and the surest sign that you have listened is to ask a follow-up question.

It may sound like a questioner could just switch to autopilot, asking open-ended question after open-ended question. Not so.

Instead of lobbing generic softballs (like *How do you feel about that?*), focus with intent on what the other person is saying, so that you can arrive at a next question that is both sensitively probing (*What did you learn from that experience?*), yet intuitively appealing to answer (*How did you meet each other?* directed at a couple). These are questions that will keep both the speaker and the listener engaged.

In his book, *The Science of Selling*, David Hoffeld explained that the human brain is hardwired to disclose information in levels – much like peeling one layer of an onion reveals another layer. Unless you ask follow-up questions, it's impossible to fully understand what the other person would like to convey in all its complexity.

Hoffeld references studies showing that when we ask follow-up questions, the other person experiences an increase in the neural activity in the areas of the brain associated with reward and pleasure.

Follow-up questions trigger the release of dopamine and oxytocin in the brains of those answering them. Effective follow-up inquiries lead to the questioner being perceived as more understanding, more caring, and a better listener.

The authors noted the proclivity of people in an initial interaction to express their own viewpoints and to self-promote. Yet those who ask more questions are thought to be more responsive and are better liked.

There's solid research demonstrating that asking a question of a person who has a negative impression of you can even turn their opinion around. The social psychologist Robert Cialdini has shown that simply asking for advice can alter a negative impression. It shows not only that you are truly interested in their point of view, but you're willing to give them the opportunity to influence your outlook.

If you find yourself asking a variation of *Is that something you might want to do again?* or *Would you do it differently the next time?,* you can be certain you are deep into excellent follow-up territory.

When you ask questions like that, your audience will be totally engaged.

What's the Point?

Active listening is about asking thoughtful questions and follow-up questions.

•Part Two•

A Simple Change in Focus with a Huge Impact

What three traits will transform your relationships?

Let your curiosity be greater than your fear.
 −Pema Chodron

Chapter Four

Can Curiosity *Feed* the Cat?

W e can pave the way to better relationships by strengthening certain traits.

Have you ever seen a well-tended garden? If you're going to train a tomato plant to grow tall and produce fruit, you need to stake it for structural support.

Certain traits – properly developed and cultivated – are the stakes that permit us to engage others.

What traits help us ask good questions? I ask a related question every time I give a talk: "What's the trait that correlates most directly with success?" Almost everyone believes it is something like "honesty," "trustworthiness," or "sincerity." These are all important traits, but they don't predict success the way *curiosity* does.

A hidden power

Nothing is more fundamental for success in almost any activity than the desire to investigate and learn more. Researchers have shown that curiosity is the fuel that powers personal growth and happiness. Curiosity also triggers neurochemical changes in our brains, priming them for learning.

George Loewenstein explained the critical importance of curiosity in a seminal paper, published in 1994. Not only did he find it was a "driving force in child development," but he also observed that being curious is "one of the most important spurs to educational attainment." Curiosity is essential for maturing into a successful adult.

The virtue of curiosity has also been extolled in the media. An article in *Time* explained that curiosity is "the engine" that powers so much of what we accomplish. Without the drive to learn, powered by curiosity, it's highly unlikely you'll succeed.

The most successful business leaders surround themselves with curious people. Companies like Google encourage their employees to be curious by devoting up to 20% of their worktime to pursuing side projects they are curious about (these forays into curiosity have produced Google Maps, Twitter, and Slack).

Curious business leaders ask a lot of questions that help them make better decisions. Leaders of these companies are less likely to search only for information that confirms their current belief. They are curious about information that contradicts what they already know. Employees who are naturally curious also perform their jobs better and have less conflict at work. They are able to foster more open communication, and are more successful as a result.

It's remarkable that curiosity is often neglected. Curiosity for its own sake has never been particularly valued. Some philosophers claim that curiosity is not that important, calling it "the most superficial of all the affections," and even neglecting to include it in the essential virtues or traits that humans should cultivate.

We don't care

What's even more remarkable about the lack of curiosity in adults is that they didn't start out that way. Children are naturally curious. They find almost everything fascinating. Have you ever gone to a grocery store with a young child? They have endless questions about the most mundane items, like

"Where do corn flakes grow?" or "Why is food put in a can?" and "Why do you have to peel a banana?"

Asking questions is not simply a case of children acquiring knowledge they don't have. They also experience a host of associated positive emotions when exploring their world through the lens of curiosity.

As we age, we become jaded. We don't have as many questions. Steve Taylor, the author of *Making Time*, sees adults as "desensitized to our experience, which means that we process less information." The sense of wonder we feel as children – being in a *state* of curiosity – is replaced by wondering that's more directly linked to our interests and personality.

We are no longer pleasantly mystified that the sky can turn so many colors at sunset. We revert to only being curious about particular activities, like playing a musical instrument or learning foreign languages, if that.

Our educational system shares the blame. Educators note the decline in the ranking of the U.S. in mathematics, which they attribute to a dearth of curiosity and a lack of a desire to learn. Observations of suburban elementary classrooms found a surprising absence of questions from kindergartners and 5th grade students. In its place was an alarming tendency to follow adult instructions robotically.

Teachers were the ones asking questions, and the students dutifully responded. Researchers concluded that "the incessant curiosity that leads to so much knowledge during the first five years of life dwindles as children go to school."

As researchers have noted, curiosity turns out to be a central pillar in the edifice of academic performance. It's the driving force behind the pleasure of learning, facilitating our desire to both crave and enjoy new information that comes our way.

That's because being curious floods our neural circuit boards with dopamine. Any sensible educational system ought to be based on cultivating the innate desire to tackle new ideas and challenging tasks. Unlike rote learning, gaining knowledge in this way makes it stick.

Instead of encouraging students to develop and pursue passions of particular interest to them, our educational system emphasizes a withering conformity.

Little curiosity; little business

There's no shortage of examples of the catastrophic consequences of lack of curiosity in corporate America.

If Excite had been curious about the possibility of making its search engine better, it might have accepted Larry Page's offer to purchase Google for $750,000 when it had that opportunity. Google is currently worth around $130 billion. Excite is rarely used as a search engine.

If Kodak had been curious about the potential of digital cameras, it would have leveraged the patent it received in 1977 for one of the first digital cameras. Instead, it continued to focus on traditional film cameras, and lost out on a massive opportunity. The once-proud company filed for Chapter 11 bankruptcy in 2012.

If Blockbuster had been curious about the possibility of online streaming, it wouldn't have turned down multiple offers to buy Netflix. Today, Blockbuster is down to its last store, while online streaming services proliferate and prosper.

If Radio Shack had been curious about e-commerce, it wouldn't have stuck stubbornly to selling exclusively from its brick-and-mortar stores. Retail has changed dramatically since the shopping malls of the 1980s, many of which are just hollowed out shells of their former selves. E-commerce entities like Amazon had Radio Shack for lunch.

Lack of curiosity wasn't the only factor in these massive corporate blunders, but it played a meaningful role.

Curiosity cookies

Fostering your curiosity has many benefits beyond being happier and more successful. It's also been found to have remarkable health benefits, like making you less prone to develop Alzheimer's disease and more likely to live longer. Your overall mental health improves if you are curious because you're much more likely to find meaning and purpose in what you do. There's also evidence that curious people are less likely to be depressed.

It's not just your mental health that improves – increasing your curiosity level can be the impetus for making healthy choices. In one experiment, people were given the choice between a healthy and an unhealthy fortune cookie. If their curiosity was first primed by being told that the healthy cookie contained a fortune customized for them, over 70 percent of participants chose the healthy cookie. When curiosity was not primed in another group by providing information about an individualized fortune, almost 80 percent chose the unhealthy cookie.

The upshot is clear. As Todd Kashdan, author of *The Power of Curiosity*, says, "One of the most reliable and overlooked keys to happiness is cultivating and exercising our innate sense of curiosity." He explains that developing a heightened sense of curiosity makes us open to different experiences, which permit us to "experience discovery, joy and delight."

Adults do have the ability to become more curious. Kashdan, in his subsequent book, *Curious? Discover the Missing Ingredient to a Fulfilling Life,* identified common traits in adults who were able to remain curious into old age. He found they chose careers that allowed them to be autonomous and independent, didn't see themselves as bound by or constricted by social norms, and most of all, had rich emotional lives that involved meaningful relationships with others.

Curious about relationships?

Curiosity should be at the top of the list of traits to develop if you want to forge deeper relationships. Scholars argue that "curiosity's connection to care and concern makes it an important component of any friendship or deep relationship." It's practically hard-wired into the meaning of the word. *Curare*, the Latin root of the word "curiosity," means "to care for."

One study showed that curious people are perceived to be more attractive to others. They also create deeper bonds than those who are not as curious. The author of the study described curiosity as "the secret juice of relationships." This is true whether you know the person you're having the conversation with, or (as another study demonstrated) whether they are a complete stranger.

When you are sincerely curious, you'll be surprised how much information people will share with you. It's this disclosure that builds more meaningful relationships. You don't just wind up feeling closer to the other person – you actually are. This is especially true for introverts or individuals who suffer from social anxiety when talking to others. Curiosity is a remarkable tonic for reducing anxiety, whether engaged in an intimate conversation, or just making small talk.

Being curious means you're fully engaged and actively listening. Curious people are much better at picking up non-verbal cues and even discerning the personality traits of others – even in brief interactions. It can also make us more empathetic, which is critical to enhancing our relationships.

Where "losers" win

I once had to interview a photographer for a project. After introducing herself, she told me she had been in the business for 20 years, and she stated emphatically, "I obviously know what I'm doing." She proceeded to explain at length why certain shots would be "terrific," sprinkling her explanations with terms like "natural lighting" and "soft focus." When she departed, she told me she looked forward to "scheduling the shoot."

Despite her competence and impressive portfolio, I didn't hire her. She didn't ask any questions about the project, and she exhibited a remarkable lack of curiosity about my needs. She left without ever uncovering a nagging worry I had about a particular aspect of the photoshoot. She could have easily uncovered it with a few simple inquiries.

Think about the thousands of interactions you've had with others. How many times have you had an experience similar to mine? I call these interactions "the battle of agendas." In the case of the photographer, she had an agenda (to demonstrate her expertise and creativity). I had mine (to get the best images that met my needs). She used our meeting to present her agenda in great detail. But she ignored mine. She may have won the battle, but she lost the business.

I'm not suggesting unbridled curiosity is always a positive force. If you are speeding down a highway and get distracted by a crash on the side of the road, your curiosity can have tragic consequences.

Sometimes curiosity *can* kill the cat.

Finding the curiosity balance

The goal of *Ask* is to make us happier by strengthening our relationships and improving our ability to communicate with others. Curiosity is central to that goal. How can we improve our level of curiosity so we don't do what the photographer did – while not going overboard?

In their paper, "Facilitating Curiosity," Todd Kashdan and Frank Fincham offer some suggestions for creating the conditions under which we will be our best and most curious selves.

1. Enter into conversations and situations with a curious mindset. Passivity toward the person you're interacting with significantly dampens your curiosity. Entering into situations with an open and inquisitive mindset directly leads to the beneficial outcomes discussed above.

If the photographer had actively engaged with me, and asked questions, she still might have wound up taking the same photos she had planned, but she likely would have discovered new information that would have led to meaningful discussions about the project.

2. Prepare so that you feel competent enough to be properly curious. Displaying competence in the questions you ask doesn't just result in discovering what you want to know. It also leads to praise and affirmation, which are big drivers for curiosity. Come to the conversation ready to ask relevant questions.

The photographer was on autopilot from the moment she shook my hand. She hadn't done her homework. If she had prepared for our meeting, asked relevant questions, and then appropriate follow-up questions, she likely would have won my business.

3. Start with the intention to make an emotional connection. It makes the person you're talking to relax and feel safe in your presence.

When I meet someone new, my first thoughts are: Who is this person? How did he or she become the person they are? What has been their life's journey? Every person has a story. I genuinely and sincerely want to hear it. There's nothing *I* can say that I don't already know. But everything someone tells me about them is new information.

At a recent social gathering, I met a retired executive in charge of public relations at a Fortune 500 firm. I asked him to tell me the kinds of situations he found most challenging. He told me it was when the company was faced with a potential PR disaster. I asked him to give me examples. I followed up by inquiring how he handled those events and why his approach was effective. I later discovered he thought I was very interesting – even though all I did was ask questions.

It's all about being curious.

What's the Point?

Being the most curious person in the room will result in interesting conversations and better relationships.

There's zero correlation between being the best talker and having the best ideas.
—Susan Cain

Chapter Five

Where Are You on This Spectrum?

I want to share a story with you about a trait of mine. I have a fair amount of experience speaking to audiences. It can still be intimidating at times, but I've done it so often I'm now comfortable.

After these events, I'm frequently asked to stick around and attend a post-conference networking session and dinner. While talking to a large group is no problem, interacting with hundreds of people in short bursts of conversation is stressful for me. Add live music, boisterous drinking, and the noise level in a cavernous reception hall, and I feel a pressing need to exit. As soon as I can, I beat a hasty retreat to my hotel room, where I immediately feel relaxed and re-energized.

When I share that story with extroverts, they completely gel with how great I feel speaking in front of an audience, but are puzzled by what happened at the reception. When I tell the same story to introverts, they understand why I retreated to the serenity of my hotel room during the networking session, but can't relate to how I enjoy speaking to an audience.

Whether you're an introvert or an extrovert says a lot about the way you'll react in social situations. It also impacts the way you'll build better personal relationships.

The core of your personality

All relationships benefit from mutual respect and understanding. If you want to understand yourself and others, there's arguably nothing more important than knowing whether you're an introvert or an extrovert. Susan Cain, author of the seminal book, *Quiet: The Power of Introverts in a World that Can't Stop Talking,* puts it this way: "Introversion and extroversion go to the heart of who a person is: how they work, how they live, and how they interact."

The distinction between introverts and extroverts has its roots in the work of the psychologist Carl Jung, who defined the terms based on the source of an individual's energy or motivation. In his view, extroverts were expressive and derived their energy from interaction with others. Introverts were reserved and found their energy by turning inward.

This distinction picked up steam in the 1960s with the dissemination of the Myers-Briggs Type Indicator, a widely used personality test that included categories of extroversion and introversion. It contrasted whether you "like to spend time in the outer world of people and things (extroversion), or in your inner world of ideas and images (introversion)."

There are many ways to characterize the differences between introverts and extroverts. Social situations pose a challenge to introverts, while extroverts are often the ones to organize activities, outings, and after-work parties. Extroverts are engaged in a constant search for opportunities to interact, and often are the center of attention, even in a group of strangers. Introverts rarely feel compelled to engage with others in this way.

Another way to consider the difference would be in terms of leadership. Because extroverts are more driven to being perceived as leaders, they are often assertive, goal-focused, and can sometimes be impulsive. Given these traits, it's not surprising that extroverts are more inclined to take risks than introverts. Perhaps to compensate for this tendency, extroverts enjoy sharing their problems and actively solicit advice from others.

Introverts tend to work out their problems without consulting others. They see the world in shades of gray with many uncertainties, and therefore are more cautious about risk. Introverts often don't come across initially as leaders and are reluctant to seek the limelight.

The lens of friendship is another useful way to understand the differences between introverts and extroverts. Introverts typically have few friends and don't make new friends easily. They value the ones they have, and these relationships are frequently long-standing.

Extroverts have many friendships. They're fun to be around and are often the "life of the party."

Both introverts and extroverts confront stereotyping. Because the traits of extroverts are generally more valued by society, introverts are more often perceived as being on the defensive. They may come across as distant or rude, but are more likely to be just listening intently.

Extroverts can appear brash and even insecure because of their outward nature, but that's just how they connect to others. They can be just as keen as introverts to learn new things about others.

Do you have a choice?

It might be tempting to blame an introvert or extrovert for being the way they are, but that only makes sense if they had a choice.

Studies of twins by H.J. Eysenck established early on that there was a strong genetic component to where you fell on the spectrum between introversion and extroversion. Later studies showed that lower levels of internal sensory stimulation – perhaps linked to differences in the cortical thickness in regions of the brain – might cause extroverts to seek external stimulation in ways introverts do not. Research into the genetic roots of introversion and extroversion recently took off with the introduction of functional MRIs.

Experts theorize that dopamine plays a role in explaining the difference between the way introverts and extroverts behave. Dopamine is released when we engage in activities associated with achieving a goal. The increase in the release of dopamine reinforces our enjoyment and causes us to seek out activities that will result in similar pleasurable feelings.

Neuroscientists theorize that while introverts and extroverts may experience the same levels of dopamine when engaged in these activities, extroverts appear to feel a heightened sense of reward when the dopamine is paired with the presence of specific genes. There may be something hardwired in their brain that rewards them for new experiences and risky behaviors.

The pleasure introverts derive from being alone may be explained by another neurotransmitter called acetylcholine. While dopamine may give extroverts an enhanced "high" when they interact socially or take risks, acetylcholine makes introverts "feel good when they turn inward." For introverts, acetylcholine may be the neurotransmitter of choice, rewarding them for reflective thought and focused attention.

While the research in these areas is only in its infancy, one thing is clear. You're no more responsible for the kind of brain you were born with than you are for the number of hairs on your head. All you can do is work with what you've got and do the best you can.

Where do you stand?

You probably know whether you're an extrovert or introvert. If you still need guidance, consider which one of these descriptions better fits your personality:

- I'm seen as a "people person" who gets my energy from active involvement in events. I'm excited when around other people and I like making things happen. I feel comfortable in groups and like working in them. Before I start a project, I sometimes forget to stop and understand what I want to do and why.

This description is indicative of extroverts.

- I'm seen as a "reflective" person who gets energy from dealing with ideas. I prefer doing things alone, but not without taking time to consider all the options. I feel comfortable having just a few friends and like things I can do on my own. Sometimes, I can reflect too much and take action too slowly.

This description is indicative of introverts.

At the extremes, the differences between introverts and extroverts are pronounced. But it turns out that most of us aren't at one end of the spectrum or the other. Not all extroverts party every night; not all introverts live relatively isolated lives.

As with other continuous measurements like height, where there is the occasional very tall or very short person, most people fall somewhere along a bell-shaped distribution curve. This has led many psychologists to suggest there are no pure types, and that more likely than not, many of us are "ambiverts" – able to tap into both sides of our personality as needed.

It's more nuanced

Susan Cain is absolutely right when she says that introverts and extroverts take "dramatically different approaches to work and social processes." Some people dive into their work and complete it quickly. Others are more deliberate.

Extroverts appear comfortable taking more risks and multitasking. Introverts tend to be single-minded and focused. Extroverts enjoy being in a group and voicing their opinions. Introverts are quickly drained by big gatherings and loud noise.

A closer look reveals a more nuanced reality. It might *seem* like extroverts get energy from social interactions and introverts are severely taxed by them. But, as the organizational psychologist Adam Grant points out, this is actually false. Introverts experience happiness the same way as extroverts from social interactions. It's the *kinds* of social interactions that differ: introverts thrive on one-on-one conversations. Extroverts find groups of people more stimulating.

Here's another nuanced wrinkle. It's widely believed that introverts loathe public speaking engagements and extroverts look forward to these opportunities.

There's a deep truth to that claim: studies show that introverts do feel a great deal more anxiety than extroverts at the prospect of speaking. But it doesn't follow that all introverts are bad public speakers (or all extroverts are good public speakers). In fact, some of the best public speakers have introverted personalities, but have learned how to desensitize themselves to their fear of public speaking over time. As author Malcolm Gladwell said, "Speaking is not an act of extroversion.... It's a performance." The best performers can be extroverts or introverts.

Consider another commonly held belief: extroverts make the best leaders. This claim doesn't hold up under close scrutiny. Evaluating *who* is being led might determine who might be the best kind of leader for that particular group.

If the team is a group of introverts, choosing an introvert as their leader could have a limiting effect on productivity. They may need to be encouraged to share their opinions in group meetings, which can otherwise be dominated by extroverts. An extroverted leader is the logical choice, but one who would give introverts time to think and reflect before scheduling meetings to exchange ideas. A group of extroverts might benefit from the wisdom and serenity of an introverted leader.

The reality is that both introverts and extroverts can make great leaders. Just ask Bill Gates and Mark Zuckerberg, two of the richest introverts in the world. But consider as well the impact an extrovert like Steve Jobs made on the technology sector.

What you don't know can hurt you

Given the profound impact being an introvert or an extrovert has on your behavior, it's surprising so many people are ignorant of this personality trait in others.

If you are an introvert, there are many adjustments you can make to relate effectively to extroverts. Instead of declining invitations to every social event, be selective and cope by arriving late or leaving early. When interacting with an extrovert, let them talk while you think. This plays to both your strengths.

Extroverts also need to develop coping strategies for dealing with introverts. They need to avoid confusing silence, lack of emotion, or lack of participation by others, with indifference. Introverts respond well to being asked questions rather than being expected to volunteer input. Avoid pushing them to take positions or express feelings when you sense their reluctance.

It's not just about you

Who you are is only half the equation when it comes to a relationship. When you meet someone, give some thought to whether they are an introvert or an extrovert. It can go a long way towards fashioning a deeper, more satisfying connection.

There are some signals that can aid you. The introverted person may have a slight hesitancy in manner, often a less firm handshake, and almost always a more restrained facial expression. The extrovert may appear confident and exuberant, with a firm grip and an enthusiastic smile.

At its core, *Ask* is about eliciting information, and doing so from an introvert isn't easy. Introverts often don't like to talk about themselves, so asking open-ended questions like *Tell me about yourself* might result in empty replies like *What would you like to know?* It's code for *I don't like talking about myself, but if there's something specific you'd like to know, tell me what it is and I'll respond.*

Introverts won't voluntarily contribute a lot, preferring instead to listen. If the conversation occurs in a group, they are more likely to be overwhelmed by the noise, and not say anything at all. Because they tend to think before they speak, give them a little longer to respond,

I joke that when you ask an extrovert to *Tell me about yourself,* their first thought is *How much time do you have?* You'll have no trouble getting them to open up, but that's not the same as getting to know them. Asking questions, and thoughtful follow-up questions, can help you deepen your relationship with extroverts.

If your personality traits are so deeply interwoven into the fabric of who you are, it may seem illogical to suggest to an extrovert that they have the ability to focus on the other person (or that an introvert can overcome their aversion to focusing on others as well). But researchers have shown that we are able to suspend our personality traits and adopt another if we care deeply about a project or idea.

If you're an introvert, but your extroverted partner or spouse is enthusiastic about salsa dancing, you can "act" as an extrovert in order to be supportive of their interest, and recharge later. Similarly, extroverts can defer their goal (decline an invitation to a cocktail party) in order to advance the interests of an introverted spouse or partner by spending more time at home.

We can be motivated to act "out of character" by a desire to please a loved one or something else we perceive as valuable (like advancing our careers).

Whether you are an introvert or extrovert, embrace who you are while still being sensitive to other personality types. Many introverts wish they could be more outgoing, more charismatic, and feel more comfortable contributing to conversations in a lively and engaging way. Many extroverts admire the outward calm and confidence projected by introverts and their ability to spend time assiduously working through complex problems.

Asking questions can help introverts and extroverts make a close connection to those they care about. As Carl Jung observed, "The meeting of two personalities is like the contact of two chemical substances: if there is any reaction, both are transformed."

What's the Point?

An understanding of where you and others fit on the introvert-extrovert spectrum can enhance your relationships.

Sincerity makes the very least person to be of more value than the most talented hypocrite.
−Charles Spurgeon

Chapter Six

Are You for Real?

A well-developed sense of curiosity and an awareness of where individuals lie on the extroversion-introversion spectrum isn't enough if your interest isn't genuine. The third (and arguably most critical) trait is sincerity. Without genuine sincerity backing up your actions when implementing *Ask*, you won't enjoy the benefits of a healthier and stronger relationship.

This isn't just the Golden Rule repackaged, or a plea not to misuse *Ask* in a manipulative and devious way. It goes to the heart of this book. Changing your relationships will require a fundamental commitment to implementing the steps spelled out in the next Chapters.

You won't succeed without being sincere.

You know it when you see it

Sincere people are free of hypocrisy and embody a transparent honesty they wear on their sleeve in a non-boastful way. The critic Lionel Trilling described it as a match between what you are saying and what you are feeling. Implicit in that notion is a commitment to honesty. Yet sincerity also goes beyond mere honesty. A sincere person shares hard truths in a way that is sensitive to the feelings of others.

The clearest impact of sincerity is that it reduces stress in relationships by eliminating the need to look for subtext or "read between the lines." Our radar for picking up white lies is quite nuanced.

In a study on sincerity, researchers played recorded responses to questions like *What do you think of my new hairdo?* Some of the responses reflected the honest views of the speaker. Others had the responder reading from a script. Listeners were generally able to distinguish sincere from insincere responses.

Because sincere people are not trying to impress others, they have no problem admitting responsibility for mistakes, and don't waste time and energy trying to present themselves to others as "perfect."

Sincere individuals are also supremely confident. That doesn't mean they don't acknowledge it's normal to have fears and concerns – just the opposite. Because they fundamentally know who they are and what they stand for, they don't require the approval of others. They also aren't defensive when others disagree with them, even if their views are in the minority.

Sincere people are secure in their own skin and don't form opinions based on what's popular. They make decisions based on their own independent evaluation.

Don't extol the virtue of authenticity

Although they're often used interchangeably, there's an important difference between being "sincere" (honestly expressing your feelings to others), and being "authentic" (being true to yourself).

A person can be "authentic" if they live a life true to themselves, like someone who chooses an "off the grid" lifestyle because of a desire to protect the environment. Yet according to David Sudar, a former Buddhist monk and meditation teacher, you can be authentic and still be selfish and thoughtless, as long as you're being "true to yourself." As Sudar aptly observes, you can "authentically be a total jerk."

You can be authentic yet lack confidence, shirk responsibility for your actions, and not be honest. That's because, while sincerity requires being truthful to others, authenticity means simply being who you want to be. It's hard to fail to be authentic. No matter what happens, you can always say you were just being yourself. But if you are genuinely sincere, you take into consideration the thoughts and feelings of others. You are warm and considerate and internalize the perspectives of others.

Sincerely successful

It's not hard to identify examples of insincerity that pervade our lives: the car salesman who is focused on his commission rather than meeting your needs; the insurance person who recommends a policy that pays the biggest commission; the stockbroker who pushes products to meet a sales goal; and even the doctor who may receive direct or indirect benefits from recommending one medication over another. Modern advertising is designed to sell a product you absolutely, positively "need."

What's remarkable is the overwhelming evidence about the importance of sincerity in business. It doesn't matter what industry you're in. Without sincerity, it's almost impossible to forge a genuine connection with your customer.

One study found that clients who viewed their real estate agent as being sincere (via body language, voice tone, and facial expressions) were much more likely to feel satisfied with the service provided than those who dealt with agents they perceived as insincere.

Another study found that in order for pharmacists to succeed, it wasn't enough to provide high-quality service (though that's critical in a field where one mistake could lead to someone's death). For long-term sustainable success, they needed to develop that sense of trust with their customers through conveying sincerity.

Edward C. Bursk, formerly the editor of the *Harvard Business Review,* has given this approach a name, saying, "Sincerity is at the very crux of *low pressure selling.*"

It's not just on the sales side that sincerity matters. Researchers have shown that sponsorships of sports teams only benefit the company if the relationship is seen as genuine, and the sponsor's motives sincere. If the fit between team and company is contrived, attitudes toward the sponsor turn sour and purchases plummet.

It's also been shown the best managers are those who don't merely appear sincere when they solicit feedback, but who actually *are* sincere. Stephen J. Dubner, co-author of *Freakonomics: A Rogue Economist Explores the Hidden Side of Everything,* believes sincerity is "the biggest single thing that I've seen" that makes a leader successful.

I'm sorry

Sincerity also plays a critical role in re-establishing trust once it's been broken. Considerable attention has been given to the question of how business leaders can move on from mistakes by issuing apologies. The research is clear: apologies only work when they are sincere.

For example, in one study individuals were given three dollars to watch videos of CEOs issuing apologies. They then could wager any of their earnings and double their money by "betting" whether the CEO was in fact sincere, and the mistake apologized for was resolved. While participants in the study could not consciously point to what about the apologies was sincere or insincere, their subconscious (in the form of the neuro- and physiological responses researchers were measuring) was much better than average at picking out those apologies that *weren't* sincere.

We intuitively determine whether an apology is sincere, even if we can't articulate why.

Researchers have conducted experiments that offer compelling insights into what it is that makes an apology sincere. One meta-study unpacked the component parts of a sincere apology, noting that you don't just admit you are responsible, but you also acknowledge the severity of the transgression and explain why it happened.

When apologizing sincerely, you shouldn't speak in vague generalities, but personalize the apology and indicate what steps will be taken in the future to prevent what caused the need for an apology. Furthermore, how soon the apology was delivered, who initiated the apology, and the motivation for apologizing were all key elements in determining whether an apology was considered genuine.

Sincere love

What's true in the corporate world is doubly so in relationships. Insincerity is a relationship-killer.

If you've spent any time connected to another person, you're bound to have come into conflict and said or done something hurtful. Studies have shown that there's only one thing the offending partner can do in this situation to be genuinely forgiven: offer a sincere apology.

Yet apologies are a two-way street. If you're the one who has been wronged, you can compound the damage to your relationship by not being sincere in your forgiveness. Researchers have determined that the more sincere the apology, the more sincere the forgiveness. Sincerity breeds more sincerity.

A thoughtful apology builds trust. A healthy relationship is, at its core, based on trust. Trust is closely related to sincerity. *Ask* is about showing a sincere and genuine interest in others. Doing so builds trust and allows relationships to grow and depth to emerge.

An important link

Researchers discovered a clear link between trust and sincerity in the following experiment. Participants were told that videos they recorded would be used to raise funds for a charity. One group was advised they would receive a financial incentive based on the amount of money raised by their video. The other group wasn't told anything about incentives, but merely told their video would support the charity.

When the videos were shown to potential donors, even though they didn't know which group was incentivized, they could sense it. Donors gave less money to the incentivized group, somehow correctly perceiving them as being less trustworthy than those who weren't incentivized. These results have been confirmed multiple times.

You can't fake sincerity

I once observed a trial where the entire verdict was altered by the jury's sense that the attorney for the defendant was insincere. I was scheduled to try a case before the same judge and wanted to observe how she conducted a trial.

A Fortune 500 company was being sued for sex discrimination. Their attorney apparently decided to "dress down" in order to relate better to members of the jury. He appeared each day in conspicuously inexpensive-looking, drab suits, accessorized with an outdated tie and wearing worn, unpolished shoes.

It didn't work. The jury rendered a large judgment against his client.

I was told by one of the lawyers who interviewed the jury that they found the dress of the lawyer off-putting and manipulative. They expected a large company with top-flight lawyers to look the part, and felt this lawyer was trying to deceive them. This perception impacted their assessment of his overall credibility. Researchers have confirmed that sincerity is critical in situations involving considerations of fairness.

The lawyer wearing the inexpensive suit would have been more effective if he had followed the example of prominent attorneys from Chicago who represented the victim of traumatic brain injury suffered in a trucking accident. The trial was held in a small town in South Dakota. The defendant (the trucking company) was represented by local lawyers, who emphasized to the jury that the plaintiff (the injured person) was represented by "big city" lawyers.

Instead of trying to downplay or avoid mentioning their "big-city" status, the plaintiff's lawyers embraced it. They told the jury their client deserved the same top-drawer legal representation someone from a big city would receive. If jurors thought someone from a small town deserved less, they could reduce the award.

The jury returned a huge verdict for their client.

Substance over form

The lawyers in the South Dakota case didn't just dress the part. That would be simply catering to the *appearance* of sincerity. They did the number-one thing you can do to show you're sincere: *they asked questions*. They didn't tell the jury what to think. They asked them if they thought it was unfair that an injured party might receive a lower award solely because they lived in a small town rather than in a big city. They asked if rural Americans were entitled to the same level of legal representation as the wealthy.

By asking questions instead of making statements, the lawyers displayed trust in the judgment of the jury. The questions gave members of the jury a feeling of importance and showed their opinion was valued.

If improving your relationships matters to you, then shift from a self-centered agenda to sincerely caring about others. That is the ultimate value of sincerity.

Being sincere represents a choice to care about what *really* matters and what actually makes us happy – our relationships with others.

What's the Point?

Sincerity is central to generating trust, and is crucial for healthy, meaningful relationships.

•Part Three•

Wait Till You Hear This!

What's required to fundamentally change the way you communicate?

People often think they're talking to each other,
when they're really talking past each other.
– Judith E. Glaser

Chapter Seven

Is It All about You?

Better conversations lead to better relationships. What's remarkable is how few of us have an understanding of what a good conversation looks like.

Most people think they are pretty good at conversation. That's certainly what I used to believe. I didn't need to think about it – conversations just happened naturally. They were spontaneous outpourings where I said whatever was on my mind, and the other person did the same.

I never gave a thought about planning for a better conversation. My "plan" was simply to do what I always did: share my thoughts, demonstrate my expertise, or entertain by discussing my experiences.

The research I uncovered turned all that on its head.

More about me?

Communication is what separates us as a species. While animal communication may have superficial similarities to human language, humans clearly are different. Our minds are unique, as evidenced by our intelligence, our foresight, and especially by the way we express ourselves.

We spend most of our working day communicating with others. By some estimates, talking to others accounts for up to 80% of our workday. A relatively small percentage of our in-person conversations involve seeking the input of others.

This imbalance is exacerbated when we communicate digitally. Platforms like Twitter, Facebook, Instagram, WhatsApp, Viber, Hangouts, Snapchat and many others don't just facilitate talking about ourselves – they make it almost irresistible.

An analysis of Twitter messages found the percentage of communications focused on ourselves approached 80%. Sharing information about ourselves was so prevalent that researchers coined a new term, "meformers" (as contrasted with "informers"), to describe those creating this content.

In both our personal and digital contacts, we're primarily communicating *our* thoughts, about *ourselves*, and conveying *our* agenda. The person we are supposed to be communicating with? They've been left in the dust.

It feels so good

In my interactions, I never thought about whether I was talking about myself, conveying information, giving advice or simply listening. I rarely asked questions.

There are many reasons why we don't ask questions, from the mistaken belief by business executives that doing so is inefficient, to fear of ceding control (and the floor) to others. We deeply believe what we have to say is important.

We have a proclivity to talk about ourselves because of the mistaken belief that it increases our likeability, or the hope that people will ask us questions. We're not just blithely yammering away – we really do think talking more will impact others positively.

There's an even more basic explanation for why we seemingly can't stop talking: at their very core, our brains are hard-wired to talk about ourselves.

Why? Because when we talk about ourselves, we release the highly pleasurable hormones of dopamine and oxytocin.

It's chemical.

An epiphany from Harvard

In a study published in Proceedings of the National Academy of Sciences, Diana I. Tamir and Jason P. Mitchell, who were then researchers from the Harvard University Social Cognitive and Affective Neuroscience Lab, published findings of their investigation concerning how self-disclosure impacted "neural and cognitive mechanisms associated with reward."

The Harvard researchers were familiar with studies showing that a certain system in the brain responds positively to the anticipation of reward. This system is called the mesolimbic dopamine system. Previous studies demonstrated these parts of the brain reliably activate in response to rewards like food, money, learning that others share an opinion similar to yours, or even "catching a brief glimpse of an attractive member of the opposite sex."

Building on this work, the Harvard study used functional magnetic resonance imaging to investigate whether talking about yourself activates reward-linked regions of the mesolimbic dopamine system. Not content to find out if talking about yourself releases dopamine and oxytocin, they added an interesting wrinkle to the experiment.

Participants were asked to bring a friend or relative to the laboratory, and then, while inside an MRI scanner that measured their brain activity in real time, they alternatively shared their own opinions and attitudes, discussed the opinions of others, or answered a trivia question. When they disclosed their opinions, they were then told whether their responses would or would not be shared with the friend or relative they brought to the lab.

The findings were stunning.

The researchers discovered that when participants talked about themselves – even when they didn't think anyone else would share in these disclosures – there was "robust activity in those neural regions implicated in reward processing." Those parts of the brain associated with highly pleasurable activities lit up. When they engaged in the alternate activities, the brain wasn't comparably activated. For each activity, the participants were given a different monetary reward.

Participants were willing to sacrifice a higher monetary reward (about 17 percent of earnings) to engage in self-disclosure.

Talking about yourself is "intrinsically rewarding," even if nobody is listening.

Brain activation in these reward regions was even *more* pronounced when participants were told their answers would be shared with their friend or relative. Knowing someone is listening when we're talking about ourselves even more strongly activates parts of the brain crucial for feelings of reward and pleasure. There was no evidence of a similar response when the participants discussed the opinions of others.

Dopamine, and arguably oxytocin, flood our system when we have an audience. No wonder we talk about ourselves.

Before you conclude this study is an outlier, consider what the sociologist Charles Derber found in a study of over 1500 interactions. While few of us would self-identify as conversational narcissists, in his book, *The Pursuit of Attention*, Derber found almost everyone in a conversation sought to redirect attention to themselves and their experiences. This is not surprising once you understand brain chemistry: it feels really good to talk about ourselves.

Give the "high" to others

If talking about ourselves releases powerful hormones that make us feel great, then two people conversing can become a turf war – the battle of agendas I discussed earlier. Each party to the conversation wants the "microphone" so they can achieve the hormonal high. When this occurs, according to Judith Glaser, author of *Conversational Intelligence*, you're no longer having a conversation. You are talking past each other. A monologue is not a dialogue.

Based on the Harvard study, we now understand what's going on with the brain of the person doing the talking. It's on fire. What about the brain of the listener? Glaser notes the brain disconnects "every 12 to 18 seconds" to process the conversation. The other person may be spending as much time with their own thoughts as they are listening to what you are saying.

It gets worse.

If the person listening interprets what's being said as a rejection of them – if you rarely check in with them other than to get minimal confirmation that they are listening -- then they soon might feel "cut off, invisible, unimportant, minimized or rejected."

As a result, quite a different hormone is released into their brains – the stress hormone cortisol. When it's released in large amounts, it can shut down their prefrontal cortex – the part of the brain that processes information rationally.

Now the limbic brain – known as the emotional brain – takes over. The listener will feel anxious and stressed and may react the way we do when confronted with dangerous situations.

The asymmetry between what is happening for the speaker and listener is quite telling. The brain of the listener isn't getting the benefit of an inflow of pleasurable sensations from the dopamine reward system the way the speaker is. The neurochemicals they are experiencing are the same ones released when we are in physical pain.

It's doubtful you intend your conversation to cause pain, anxiety and stress, yet that's precisely what occurs if you are doing the majority of the talking.

No one wants to hear "your story"

One of the biggest traps about having meaningful conversations is that you should "tell your story" – those anecdotes about your life experiences that you believe others will find interesting. There's no shortage of advice encouraging you to tell your story to anyone who'll listen. The theory is your story makes you different and unique, and it's essential to share it so others will appreciate you for the special person you are.

The benefit of telling your story is particularly extolled for those in business – especially if they are selling a product or service. Salespeople are encouraged to tell stories that will make an emotional connection with prospects, or solve a customer's potential problem, or overcome an objection. Even American Express has hopped on the "tell your story" bandwagon. It believes customers "love to hear a good story," and that "telling stories is one of the most important tools for marketing a company's product."

Often, advocates for telling stories rely on neuroscience for justification. They note that "our brains love good storytelling," and that doing so releases oxytocin.

They are right. Your story is powerful and does release pleasurable hormones – *in you.*

That's not the only problem. Telling your story means you are speaking and the other person is listening. This is the perfect storm for a *non-productive* conversation, akin to a stress-inducing monologue.

Imagine a different story-telling scenario: instead of telling *your* story, you focus on asking the other person about *their* story. Instead of doing all the talking, you listen carefully and then ask thoughtful follow-up questions.

Now the other person gets to experience all the benefits of talking about themselves. Because you're actively listening and participating through questions, you don't experience stress. It's a "win-win."

You'll be amazed at how easy it is to empower others to talk about themselves. Their brains are enjoying the release of "happiness molecules" that come from sharing their story.

You'll be amazed by what you hear. You'll also learn a lot because, when others share their stories, they're adding to your knowledge and enhancing your experience.

What about me?

While there are many benefits to asking questions, there are some barriers to overcome. The biggest one is the lack of reciprocity. You'll find no matter how many questions you ask, and regardless of the amount of time the other person talks, rarely will you experience a reciprocal interest in you and your life. You probably won't be asked to share your story.

Once they start talking about their lives, people are reluctant to turn off the powerful, positive feelings they experience. Having someone ask about their life is such a rare occurrence, it's unlikely they'll "yield the floor."

Something interesting happens when you cede the floor, and instead focus on the other person. While they won't even realize that you're not talking much, what they *will* realize is that they are having a very meaningful conversation with someone who they now regard as very special and intensely curious – *you*.

The price of being the recipient of those positive feelings and characterizations is giving up the opportunity to talk about yourself.

It's well worth it.

Try this at home

When I tell people the key to deepening relationships is asking open-ended questions without trying to steer the conversation, to offer nothing declarative (unless asked), and to expect little reciprocity, they are understandably skeptical. Here's an exercise I tell them to try at home to overcome their initial reluctance.

When you are with someone you love, ask questions. If they ask you how your day was, respond as follows: *Great. What about yours?* When they respond, keep asking nice follow-up questions (*What was that like? Would you do that again? Why do you think you enjoyed it so much?*). The more you do it (always in an honest and sincere way), the better, more meaningful, and deeper your relationship will be.

Most people resist engaging in this exercise. They're concerned this departure from the way they usually relate (presumably where they dominate the conversation) will result in the other person saying something like *What's wrong with you? Why are you asking me so many questions?*

But if your questions are open-ended and non-threatening, this reaction is rare. The other person's brain is flooded with dopamine and oxytocin. They're feeling happy. They're so preoccupied with this positive feeling, they won't notice you are showing much more of a genuine and authentic interest in them than normal.

If you're reluctant to start the process at home, then start a conversation with a stranger. It can be in a hotel elevator, while shopping, or while waiting for an appointment with a service professional. It's easy to do. Comment on the weather, or compliment them on their clothes, or ask them where they're from. When they respond, ask an open-ended question (*Have you lived there long? Do you always shop at that store? What do you do?).* Let the conversation go wherever it flows.

When it ends, note whether the other person asked you *any* questions. Most likely they didn't. Instead of focusing on what you might initially think is a negative, catalogue everything you learned. Watch their reaction. It's likely to be genuine happiness and enthusiasm. You'll quickly see that there's a lot to be gained by simply asking questions.

I tell my clients to follow two basic conversational rules if they want to fundamentally change their relationships:

1.   Don't end any sentence with a period. Instead, try and make every statement a question. This rule is easy to state, but challenging to implement because we are predisposed to convey information. You'll need to retrain your brain to suppress that inclination.

2.   Picture the forehead of other person as emitting a light. The light is green when they are talking, and red when you are talking. The goal of every conversation is to keep the green light on for as long as possible.

Master these rules and you are well on your way to better relationships.

What's the Point?

If you want to see an immediate,
transformational change in your relationships,
become the most interested person in the room,
instead of the most interesting.

Most advice is useless.
It pleases the provider more than the receiver.
It's created based on one's expectations,
not on understanding others.
– Gustavo Razzetti

Chapter Eight

What's the Best Advice about Giving Advice?

When I discuss listening more and talking less, I often hear something like the following:

I hear what you're saying, Dan. Thank goodness I don't do that. All I do is share advice when I'm asked to do so. Other times I hear them say something like, *I would never talk over people. Instead, I listen to what they have to say, and then present the facts supporting my view.*

These may seem like better alternatives to talking about ourselves. But are they really that much better?

The research says otherwise. An optimal conversation turns out not to be an agenda-driven endeavor that results in either advice or persuasion. Instead, the best conversations emerge from an open-ended exploration that doesn't seek a particular outcome.

Who wants your advice?

We are all tempted to give advice. It's practically part of human nature. Giving advice is highly pleasurable – for those giving it. I know. My entire life has involved giving advice for a fee – initially as a lawyer, then as a financial advisor, as a coach to advisory firms, and as an author. Given this background, I felt free to dispense advice in my personal life. I now understand why that's so counter-productive and ill-advised.

It might surprise you to discover just how much advice we give. It turns out to be a lot, and quite a bit of it is perhaps the most damaging kind of advice: unsolicited. There's been some very interesting research into the harm of unsolicited advice not just for the receiver (who shuts down immediately), but to the person giving it, because of the damage it does to the relationship.

When researchers looked "inside" advice, they found some interesting patterns. We are much more likely to give unsolicited advice to those we are closest to than to strangers. It's actually quite rare to hear someone pipe up in the grocery line, offering parenting advice to the person struggling to control their child. But if confronted with that same scenario with someone you know, seven times out of ten you're likely to offer your opinion – and almost always without having first sought more information.

This advice causes a lot of stress in those receiving it. And no wonder: it's not informed, it's completely unsolicited, and it's quickly offered as if the advice giver believes they are an expert.

Is your "good" advice "bad"?

The first problem in this scenario is that the advice giver is often *not* an expert. Consider the impact of the well-known "Dunning-Kruger effect," in which people believe that they give better advice than they actually do.

It's not just that we overestimate our own abilities in this regard. What's worse is that we are so busy giving (bad) advice that we can't step back and recognize that's what we are doing.

This combination of low self-awareness combined with the lack of information required to offer informed advice is lethal when it comes to what we value most: healthy relationships.

When you tell someone "how to live," you position yourself as the "professional" voice of authority. You would be better off just trying to be a friend. In fact, the research says it's taking this authoritative stance that leads to resistance in others.

Often the advice being given structurally differs widely from what is needed. When you give advice, you are often removed from the situation, which makes you view it in more abstract terms. The advice giver tends to prescribe advice that is more idealistic than pragmatic. The focus is more on the "whys," when what is needed is "how" information.

Advisers relentlessly push their agenda, offering multiple reasons in favor of acting idealistically – even though by this point in the "conversation," the recipient of the advice has long stopped listening.

A relationship killer

If you really want to improve a relationship, shift your focus from giving advice to listening. Imagine a situation where your child just graduated from college. She comes to you and says, *I'm thinking of taking a year off to "find myself." Maybe I'll bum around Europe or take some courses that interest me, or both. What do you think?*

Instead of driving a truck through the opening she's given you, ask questions like *Tell me more about your thought process. What triggered your consideration of this option?* Her response to these questions will tell you a lot, and may even indicate she's considered all the issues you were about to raise.

When you rush to provide advice, you're unlikely to be addressing the real issue, since you don't have an understanding of the context. The research is clear: You can only give helpful advice when you understand the perspective of the other person. The kind of egocentric mindset inherent in advice giving is what makes the advice so bad. It doesn't incorporate the other person's perspective. It quickly escapes our lips before we can even gather information.

A while back, a friend, who's a very talented executive with a graduate degree in finance, had a dental procedure. The day after the procedure, he called to tell me he was experiencing unexplained bruising under his eye. Without hesitation, I said, "Maybe you should check with your dentist." He dryly replied, "Thanks for that suggestion, Dan. I hadn't thought of that."

He was correct. My "advice" was useless and obvious.

We want to feel our advice is making a positive contribution but, in fact, the message (intentional or not) is that the other person is pretty stupid not to have considered our option. Advice offered in the heat of the moment is rarely adopted and almost always viewed as an intrusion. Even when people appear to be asking for your advice, they are more likely seeking validation of a decision they've already made.

A dead end

How many times have you had this experience? You're talking to someone about an issue important to both of you. You have a strong disagreement. You each explain the logic behind your conflicting views. At the end of the discussion, one of you looks at the other and says, *Before I heard your reasoning, I was in complete disagreement with your position. Now that I understand better, I have come around to your view.*

If the answer is "never," you're not alone. I've made that inquiry to thousands of people. The question alone gets a laugh. It turns out that behind the laughter is solid science. There's research showing persuasive explanations are not "transportable," meaning it's difficult for us to persuade others through our narratives. Why then do we waste time – and undermine our relationships – trying to persuade others we are "right" and they are "wrong"?

Comedian George Carlin famously observed, "Anyone driving slower than you is an idiot and anyone going faster than you is a maniac." His sage humor illustrates a concept known as "naïve realism." In short, our take on reality is strongly influenced by our perception.

Here's an example of naïve realism at work in a low-stakes disagreement of the kind that is common in relationships. My wife and I don't argue much, but there's one area where we often disagree. She prefers the air conditioning set to a level I find uncomfortably cold. It's obvious that my preferred temperature is the "right" one and hers isn't. Why can't she see that?

Numerous studies, summarized in Thomas Gilovich and Lee Ross's *The Wisest One in the Room,* indicate the pervasiveness of "naïve realism." In one remarkable study, participants were shown two videos of a demonstration. Half the participants were told it showed demonstrators protesting abortion outside an abortion clinic. The other half were told the demonstrators were protesting the military's "don't ask, don't tell" policy outside a recruitment center.

The two videos were in fact *identical* – the only difference was what the viewers were told regarding the subject matter of the protests. All the participants had previously filled out questionnaires providing insight into their views on these subjects. Both groups were then asked whether the protesters violated a law that prohibited access to facilities.

The opinion of the participants on the legality of the conduct of the protesters "depended on the congruence of the protestors' positions with the subjects' own cultural values." The majority of those who were pro-choice believed the protestors were blocking access to the clinic. Similar results were found in those who were told the video was taken in front of a military recruitment center.

As Gilovich and Ross convincingly demonstrate, our view of the world is not the truth per se, but a perspective that has been shaped by our own vantage point, history, and idiosyncratic knowledge. Since each of us perceives the world through the prism of our biases, efforts to persuade others to abandon their perspective – their past – is doomed to fail.

You can save a lot of time, effort and frustration by accepting this reality.

Fighting facts

There's good evidence that trying to persuade someone releases stress hormones like cortisol and adrenaline. Adrenaline increases their heart rate and blood pressure, and cortisol spikes their blood sugar, weakens their immune system, and puts their brain on high alert.

Trying to persuade is the perfect storm for causing the release of these stress hormones. Not only are you putting someone in a position where they have little control, but you are creating a situation that is threatening to their ego by challenging their competence.

We often try to persuade using logic. We believe that, if the facts are on our side, we will be effective at convincing others we are "right." This approach is fraught with problems.

It assumes we all see the issue in the same way. Naïve realism teaches us that we perceive situations through a lens of our own biases. We aren't starting from the same perspective.

Even if you could overcome this obstacle, you'll find that people don't *process* information objectively. A number of subconscious factors impact our decision-making process.

One of these factors is the "rule of consistency." It holds that once you make up your mind about something, it's very difficult to change it. You are almost automatically programmed to stick with the way you've been doing things, even when it no longer makes sense. The rule of consistency explains why Apple users are so loyal to the brand and unwilling to consider newer Android devices that might have superior features.

When I was an investment advisor, I used to convey the overwhelming data supporting index-based investing to investors who typically were trying to "beat the market" by market timing and stock picking. I would show them that over a 10 or 15-year period, more than 80% of active mutual fund managers underperformed their index benchmark, and that it was very difficult to identify prospectively those funds likely to outperform.

I can't remember a single instance where I was successful in using this data to persuade a "stock picker" to become an index-based investor. Instead, the response was typically this: *You're not saying it's impossible, just that it's unlikely. Why should I assume my broker and I can't beat these odds?*

It's like magic

Here's the epiphany that changed everything for me. Understanding it is key to implementing *Ask*.

Whenever I'm engaged in a conversation, there is one incontrovertible truth: while I have little control over what the other person thinks, I have meaningful control over the feelings I create in them.

Depending on what I do and say, I can either cause dopamine or oxytocin to be released in their brains, making them feel good about themselves and me, or cause cortisol to be released, making them stressed. I can ask them questions about themselves or push my agenda. Which should I choose?

End your efforts to persuade. As counterintuitive as that sounds, trying to persuade someone is exactly the wrong way to win them over.

A much better option

Picture your brain as a computer where the hard drive has been wiped clean. You won't try to entertain, educate, or charm. You won't dazzle with your expertise or steer the conversation in any direction. All that remains is genuine curiosity.

How do you go about asking questions when you've stopped offering advice or trying to persuade? When you're asked for advice, view it as an opportunity to implement empathy. Instead of advice or persuasion, train your brain to see the interaction through the prism of wanting to understand what the other person is *feeling*.

Only by offering emotional support and then actively gathering information about the situation will any advice you offer be heard. Once you go through these two steps, the person you want to persuade or advise will often find their footing and make the right decision for themselves. You can't change that decision, but you will be the beneficiary of the good feelings that flow from your willingness to help them clarify their position (when all you did was listen and ask questions).

The best advice is no advice at all. If you really want to help someone and build a better relationship, work with them as a partner towards a joint solution.

Insight from an outbreak

Here's a vivid example that illustrates this point. We are now confronting in the US a measles outbreak. It's attributable in part to the "anti-vaxxer" movement, which believes the measles, mumps and Rubella vaccine causes autism and other adverse side effects. Ten years ago, there were fewer than one hundred cases of measles in the US. In 2019, 1,281 individual cases of measles were reported in 31 states.

The overwhelming scientific evidence refutes the concerns of anti-vaxxers. By failing to vaccinate their children, these parents put vulnerable babies and adults at risk of an illness that can have serious complications.

Pediatricians find parents who raise objections to having their children vaccinated very frustrating. Many respond by spelling out these facts: If your child doesn't get the vaccination, there's a good chance they will contract the disease. These diseases can cause brain swelling, brain damage, and even death. The two-dose vaccination is 97 percent effective, and there is no credible scientific support that vaccination causes autism or damages the immune system.

Yet a comprehensive study found this data-based response wasn't effective. It recommended replacing it with an empathetic approach.

One pediatrician who was persuaded by these studies changed her tactics. She accepted the fact that "no one listens to blue-in-the-face, percentage-spewing health-care providers. People listen to health-care providers who are open-hearted and who understand them as individuals."

Instead of reviewing the data, she reassures parents that she doesn't take their position personally. She asks them to voice objections and concerns, and acknowledges the important role of parents in protecting their children. She then states she also felt anxious when her three children had vaccinations, but overcame her feelings because she had far greater worries about what might occur if they didn't.

She reported that a typical patient response is: *Thank you for your respect and understanding. I'll think about what you said and I'll be back.* She considers this a "win" because she has begun to build trust.

The next time you're tempted to dispense advice or persuade someone with facts, take off your "all-knowing dispenser of wisdom hat" and put on your "empathy hat." Your new goal is to *elicit* information. Research shows your shift will have a profound effect, generating incidental feelings of gratitude for being listened to, and ultimately making the person being asked questions more receptive to the ideas of others.

In those situations where you are tempted to give advice, first check these boxes:

- ☐ Do you fully understand the issue, or should you be asking more questions?

- ☐ Are you sure your advice is being sought, or does the other person just want to be heard?

- ☐ Can you substitute an empathetic response instead of advice?

Instead of dispensing "wisdom," ask this question: *Would it be helpful to you if I (shared my personal experience, provided data, gave you my understanding, etc.)?* When you do share your point of view, immediately follow it with questions like *Was that helpful? Do you need more details? What else can we explore?*

Asking questions substitutes empathy for advice and eliminates the counter-productive and stress-inducing activity of trying to persuade.

What's the Point?

Avoid the dual trap of giving advice and trying to persuade others you are "right."

Most people do not listen with the intent to understand.
They listen with the intent to reply.
–Stephen R. Covey

Chapter Nine

Can You Flip the Switch?

A genuine conversation is *not* about talking. It's about listening.

Talking is the big relationship killer. It's impossible to focus on others and put your agenda aside when you're internally directed.

Is it possible to flip the script in your brain and empower the other person to talk? The answer is a resounding "yes."

What if they can't talk?

What if you came home and found a loved one on the floor, barely conscious? You asked them what happened, and they struggled to respond. How intently would you be listening? How likely is it that you would interrupt them?

You would elicit information and use it to provide assistance. Your listening skills would be razor sharp. You wouldn't be thinking about your agenda.

Listening in this manner, when not absolutely necessary, is a challenge. Real communication starts with seeking to develop a deep understanding. That's the kind of listening *Ask* requires.

Here's a personal example. My wife is an artist. She has studied extensively in Florence, Italy. We have rented an apartment and lived there for extended periods of time while she took classes. If I met you, and you told me you were planning a trip to Florence, I have a number of options for how to respond.

I could ask you questions like *Tell me why you picked Florence? What will you be doing there? How long will you be staying?* Or I could say: *We have lived in Florence and know pretty much everything a tourist needs to know about the city.* I could then launch into an extended discussion of hotels, restaurants, museums, and renting a short-term apartment.

Ask is all about the first option. The second one demonstrates my knowledge and worldliness. It does little for you, unless you find some of the information helpful. I still would have been better advised to listen carefully to what you were saying, and ask questions to discover precisely what information you were seeking.

Don't kid yourself

It's almost impossible to look around and not find someone emphasizing the importance of active listening in communication. In fields like nursing and counseling and sales, to even law enforcement or the ministry, the importance placed on listening is prevalent. Yet, there is surprisingly little focus on what active listening actually is, and how those insights can be applied. Researchers have noted the dearth of theoretical and empirical investigation into the topic.

Most of us believe we are excellent listeners. The reality is quite different. One study found the average person only retains about 25 percent of what's being said. Writing in the *Harvard Business Review*, business researcher and analyst Ram Charan claimed that 25 percent of business leaders have an actual listening deficit.

Yet few people try to improve their listening skills. Part of this is confusion over the difference between hearing and listening. Hearing is the perception of sound. You can hear words without paying attention to them. Psychologist Kevin Gilliland compares hearing to "collecting data." It's a passive process where our brains aren't engaged.

"Passive listening" is easy to understand, but active listening is quite complex. At its core, active listening is an empathetic exercise – a person-centered approach where the listener tries to grasp "the speaker's own understanding of an experience without the listener's own interpretive structures intruding on his or her understanding of the other person."

By demonstrating "unconditional acceptance and unbiased reflection," active listeners earn the trust of those who are speaking by confirming their experiences, instead of imposing their own on what they are hearing. Or as one researcher humorously titled a paper, "Active Listening: more than just paying attention."

No wonder we prefer passive listening. Becoming an active listener isn't easy. You can't reach this goal if you are pushing an agenda or want to steer the conversation in a particular direction. This can be particularly challenging for those who believe there's no point to having a conversation unless it achieves their end game.

Tell me what I want to hear

A closely related phenomenon to passive listening is selective listening. It occurs when we filter opinions that differ from ours and tune them out. The problem with selective listening is that it shuts down dialogue and prevents us from empathizing. If you don't understand what someone is feeling, you can't empathize with them.

Selective listening has a sound basis in science. One study, using MRI scans, showed that participants were able to hear sounds played in both ears. Yet, when participants were directed to focus on any change in the pitch of the sound in one ear, they were able to ignore the sound in the other ear. They were engaged in selective listening.

We're all guilty of selective listening, whether it's ignoring what's being said while we focus on the end of a favorite television program, or filtering out evidence supporting a view on a "hot button" issue because we have a different opinion.

My experience trying to persuade prospects of the merits of index-based investing is a good example. I thought showing them the overwhelming odds against "beating the market" would persuade them to adopt a better approach. They tuned out that part of my presentation and focused instead on the small possibility that they could be the exception. They engaged in selective listening.

The consequences of selective listening can be life-threatening. In his book, *How Doctors Think*, Jerome Groopman gave an example of how emergency room doctors failed to recognize a patient was having a heart attack. The patient reported sharp chest pains, but he had no other symptoms and appeared healthy. The doctors "tuned out" the complaint of chest pains with tragic consequences.

Listen to love

In the context of a relationship, your long-term happiness can hinge on active listening. Researchers can accurately predict happiness within a marriage by observing whether newlyweds are active listeners. Dismissive husbands and uninterested wives don't stay married for long.

Studies have also revealed that over time, there is "slippage" with respect to listening in a relationship, with partners only half-listening to their spouses. Yet in long-standing marriages, the happiest couples are those where both partners remain active listeners. Regardless of whether the person you are listening to is just an acquaintance, a good friend, a romantic interest, or even a relative, the attention paid to them is returned ten-fold.

Listening reduces conflict, permits you to motivate others with your questions, and inspires a higher level of commitment from those you manage in the workplace. You will also be regarded as more trustworthy.

Do you have the right attitude?

So how do we get better at listening?

Adopt what researchers refer to as a "listening attitude." That attitude has been shown to have measurable impact on how good of an active listener you are. Researchers have found that people who don't have a good "listening attitude" tend to be unyielding in their views, hurry the other person when they are talking, and get irritated when they don't immediately understand the feelings of the person they are (purportedly) listening to. As a result, they see the other person from a critical point of view, and talk to them in a direct, forceful manner, in an effort to persuade.

Skillful listeners on the other hand demonstrate a remarkably different set of attitudes. They pay attention to even the unexpressed feelings of the other person, and actively summarize in their mind's eye what the other person is saying. Skillful listeners have a "person-centered attitude," and demonstrate "empathic understanding" and "unconditional positive regard" for the individual who is speaking.

You can use this research to evaluate your own listening skills and attitudes. One tool is known as the Active-Empathic Listening Scale (AELS). You can grade yourself using a scale from 1 to 7 on the accuracy of a series of questions intended to determine how well you sense, process and respond to what's being said to you.

Active listeners also behave in certain ways when they are speaking to others. They use inviting body language to signal their interest and express their understanding of what is being said. They don't yawn or stare blankly. Instead they nod, raise their eyebrows, and smile or frown appropriately. They aren't distracted. They listen attentively by allowing comfortable silences to emerge, giving the other person time to think and formulate what they want to say.

Most of all they are relaxed and confident and don't exude signs of nervousness (restless movements, finger drumming) or haste (talking fast, filling in silences). They resist the temptation to jump into the conversation with advice.

Listen-up

How can you become a better active listener?

Stop talking. We believe what we are saying is very important and interesting. The other person probably thinks the same thing about what they want to say. Instead of fighting for turf, focus on your conversational partner. Ask questions and show genuine curiosity.

Go second. In your interactions (personal and business), you have a choice when you meet someone. You can "go first" by making affirmative statements, often with some self-serving goal (like demonstrating your intelligence or expertise), or you can "go second," which involves asking questions intended to elicit information. "Going first" is a way for you to convey information, but "going second" will improve your personal and business relationships. When you're asked a question, your answer will be much more relevant.

Don't interrupt. Interrupting sends all the wrong messages. It conveys a lack of interest and a lack of respect.

There's compelling evidence men tend to interrupt women more frequently than men. One fascinating study reviewed transcripts of oral arguments before the U.S. Supreme Court. It found women justices were interrupted at a "markedly higher" rate during oral arguments than male justices. Both male justices and male attorneys interrupted women more frequently than they interrupted men. One of the co-authors of the study noted that even when women reach the pinnacle of their profession, they are still interrupted by subordinates.

Pause. How long do you wait after someone stops speaking before you jump in? Americans (and other English language speakers) are particularly impatient, leaving just a fraction of a second before they respond. What would happen if you significantly extended that period to 3-5 seconds? When you pause, it gives people time to "settle down and reflect a bit deeper." Of course people speak up because they feel that it's "their turn." But "your turn" has a different meaning now that you're following *Ask*. It's not an opportunity to seize control of the conversation. It's an invitation to ask more questions.

Show you're listening. According to Dale Carnegie, the author of the iconic book, *How to Win Friends and Influence People*, "Rapt attention is the highest form of flattery." By simply showing you're listening intently, you demonstrate genuine interest and concern.

You can demonstrate you're listening through gestures and eye-contact. You can restate or paraphrase what the speaker said to show you grasped both the content and the perspective of the speaker. Most of all, you show you're actively listening by asking questions that encourage the speaker to elaborate on his or her beliefs or feelings. This is the essence of active listening.

Your active listening can't be rote or automatic. If seen as a technique and not genuine, others will perceive it as insincere. The only true goal of active listening is "to develop a clear understanding of the speaker's concern and also to clearly communicate the listener's interest in the speaker's message."

It's a challenging goal, with a big payoff.

What's the Point?

Active listening will deepen your relationships.

•Part Four•

A Perfect Trifecta

How can we overcome basic misunderstandings we
have about others?

The sixth sense will empower your instinct endlessly if it understands the feelings. Thus the seventh sense is used to help the sixth sense in working effectively.
— Stephen Richards

Chapter Ten

Is There a Seventh Sense?

T here are at least five senses: taste, smell, vision, hearing, touch. There's debate over whether there's a sixth sense, called proprioception, which is defined as "the sense that lets us perceive the location, movement and action of parts of the body."

I'd like to propose a seventh sense: empathy. Unlike the other six, you have a lot of control over this new sense, and using it is just as important as the others for navigating the world we live in.

It's one thing to actively listen and recognize what someone is feeling. It's quite another to feel moved to act. You can remain a detached observer, neutrally absorbing what you hear, but when you genuinely empathize with someone you share their feelings – and act accordingly.

Researchers have differentiated between "perspective-taking" – the ability to rationally recognize someone else's point of view – and genuine "empathetic concern" – where you become emotionally engaged by what's happening to someone else. Someone who is good at perspective-taking could, for example, imagine how it would feel to be criticized before they actually criticized someone – but not weigh that in their decision-making process.

Perspective-takers dispassionately examine everyone's point of view in a disagreement before forming an opinion. Those who feel empathetic concern, on the other hand, get "kind of protective" of someone else when they see that person being taken advantage of.

They describe themselves as soft-hearted, with tender feelings of concern for other individuals, and will act on those feelings instead of merely observing. It's this latter viewpoint that generates genuine empathy.

It can be challenging to fully grasp the concept of empathy. It's hard to enter into and experience the thoughts and feelings of others.

Go second (again)

Part of what makes empathy difficult is our natural inclination to put ourselves first. In a graduation speech at Kenyon College, the writer David Foster Wallace described this egocentric vantage point as a "default setting" that is "hard-wired" into our consciousness at birth. "Think about it: there is no experience you have had that you are not the absolute center of," Wallace observed. "Other people's thoughts and feelings have to be communicated to you somehow, but your own are so immediate, urgent, real."

If empathy means sharing the full range of feelings of another person, then entering into their perspective is difficult when you are confronted with the incessant demands of your own viewpoint.

The proliferation of technology has further lowered our concern for others. Researchers have found that, in the last thirty years, empathy is on the decline in college students. It's no wonder why: communicating via text or e-mail is impersonal. We don't read emotions the way we do in-person, because digital communications don't include emotional signals and cues we rely on when we see someone. Interacting digitally can feel cold and impersonal.

The news isn't all bad. We can also use technology to increase our empathetic response towards others. Video games that require cooperation to succeed are actually good at increasing empathy in those that play them. With the advent of virtual reality, you can experience what it might be like to be someone else. That's a crucial first step on the path to sharing their emotional outlook.

In a recent experiment by Fernanda Herrera at Stanford University, participants either read about the plight of the homeless, or experienced what it was like to be homeless through a virtual reality experience.

When asked later if they would sign a petition to support homeless populations, the narrative-reading participants were less likely to offer support than those who had literally "taken the perspective" of those without a home. Those who had the virtual reality immersive experience also persisted in their empathetic mindset for a longer period of time.

The biggest takeaway from the experiment is that we can *learn* how to be more empathetic.

Monkey see. Monkey do

Have you ever yawned after someone else yawned, or smiled when someone smiled at you? You may have been experiencing the effects of mirror neurons.

In 1997, Italian neuroscientists in Parma tried to isolate the neuron in monkeys that controls elbow movement. They wired the monkey's brain with sophisticated sound detection equipment. The monkey was given a bowl of peanuts, and the equipment recorded the clicking sound of the elbow neuron when it reached for the bowl.

One day, a scientist felt an urge to eat a peanut himself. He reached into the cage and took a peanut from the bowl in front of the monkey. At that moment, the sound equipment recorded the activation of the elbow neuron in the monkey's brain. The monkey had not moved. He was merely observing the scientist reaching for the peanut.

Scientists trace the discovery of what are now known as "mirror neurons" to this event. Many neuroscientists believe mirror neurons explain how our brains are programmed to be empathetic. Think about the times when you have seen a loved one in pain, like when a baby is vaccinated. You can "feel" their pain because mirror neurons allow you to empathize.

The relationship between mirror neurons and empathy was validated by a study involving sixteen brave female volunteers. They received painful electrical shocks to their hands while their brains were scanned using functional MRI. Their brain images showed the activation of a particular region in their brain. They were then told their spouses were enduring similar shocks, without experiencing the shocks themselves.

When they heard that news, a similar matrix of neurons was activated in their brain. They "felt" the pain of their spouses even though they didn't experience the pain directly.

Hormonally challenged?

Becoming more empathetic doesn't require an electric shock, but it's not easy. Some even claim the neurological roots of empathy may run deeper in women than in men.

Men have higher levels of testosterone than women – ten times more, according to scientists. Women have more estrogen than men. These hormones help shape our behavior. Testosterone is linked to aggression, assertiveness, and anxiety. Estrogen is a mood stabilizer, leading to a sense of well-being and improved cognition.

There's evidence testosterone makes men less empathetic by reducing connectivity in brain regions responsible for feeling empathy. In one study, female volunteers were administered a sub-lingual dosage of testosterone. In subsequent tests, they took significantly longer to recognize emotions expressed in images than those who were given a placebo. Brain scans showed connectivity between the two areas thought to promote empathy were impaired by the administration of testosterone.

But a meta-study of the literature on sex differences in empathy found that the differences between the sexes just might be a function of the *methods* used to assess empathy. There is a theory that men are just as able as women to imagine themselves in the shoes of another. It may be that in an attempt to appear "tough," men underreport their responsivity to the emotional state of others when answering surveys about empathy, and women feel freer to report they cried (for example) when hearing about the suffering of another.

There also seems to be a relationship between oxytocin and our ability to empathize. The effects of oxytocin include a reduction in aggression and stress.

In one study, higher levels of oxytocin were shown to increase emotional empathy in healthy men. Another study found reduced empathy in neurology patients with medical conditions that impaired their oxytocin levels.

The surest way to increase oxytocin levels in others is to ask empathetic questions.

How empathetic are you?

One of the most widely used measures for empathy was developed by Professors Albert Mehrabian and Norman Epstein. They identified several triggers that illustrated the degree to which you were empathetic. For example, seeing a person alone or depressed would make an empathetic individual feel for that person.

An empathetic Caucasian male who is shown an image of a young African American man being pulled over by a Caucasian State Trooper will feel the anxiety of the driver. A less empathetic person may view the same image as a routine traffic stop. Your reaction to the suffering of animals or the elderly is another clue to whether you're empathetic.

Empathetic people care deeply about the problems of their friends. What happens to the people around them has a big impact on their mood.

The object of your empathy doesn't even have to be real. An empathetic person can get really involved in the lives of fictional characters on the screen or on the page.

Don't know, don't care

All of these concepts revolve around learning how to "put yourself into other people's shoes." That's easier to do when the person is close to us, but more challenging with a stranger. Society is built on altruistic acts of sacrifice for the greater good. But when the person you're asked to care about is not a member of your "tribe," there are countervailing forces that make it less likely you will care about or even want to help that person.

Research points to the fact that when there isn't a close bond, empathetic responses are "rare and fragile." Making the leap from seeing the pain to wanting to alleviate it becomes more difficult.

It's possible to reach beyond your tribe to embrace the perspective of a stranger. Studies of empathetic responsiveness have found that people are highly susceptible to being influenced by others.

One experiment had individuals listen to a broadcast of someone's call for help, while being told their biological response to the tape was being measured (in fact, it was not). They were then given fake "empathy scores" – half receiving high marks and half receiving low marks – and then given another opportunity to respond empathetically.

The study found simply being told you're empathetic leads to more empathy, while being told you're not empathetic suppresses your empathetic response.

There are some professions where individuals can experience compassion fatigue. For instance, there's evidence that, without intervention, empathy declines during medical training. But since empathy can be learned, a lack of sensitivity to the pain of others can be reversed.

In a study involving 100 residents, doctors taught to be more empathetic received higher patient rankings for understanding patient's concerns and making them feel comfortable.

There are other studies that show children as young as six or seven years old have the cognitive capacity not just to listen and recognize that someone else is hurting emotionally, but to do something about it.

It takes practice, but you can learn to connect your thoughts to emotions and hear what other people are feeling.

A novel approach

After a great deal of experimentation in my workshops, I've developed an approach to teaching empathy which is effective, enjoyable, and humorous. I create a scenario and ask participants to compete to see who can provide the most *non-empathetic* response.

In one example, I asked participants to deal with a colleague who comes into the office visibly upset. Her dog has recently died, and she is grieving. I challenge attendees to come up with the *least* empathetic response. Here are some of the "winners":

- *I'm a cat person.*

- *Think of how much you'll save on vet bills!*

- *Fortunately, you can always get another dog.*

In the process of coming up with absurdly "wrong" answers, people find themselves really empathizing with the individual who lost their dog. I've found that when you are told to give a non-empathetic response, it's much easier to "flip the switch" and think empathetically.

Empathy hacks

We have the potential to be highly empathetic, yet many of us fall short. The writer Roman Krznarichas offered three starting points for putting us on the empathy path:

Radical listening. When you listen without making judgments, offering advice or interrupting, you'll be perceived as more empathetic. One researcher found that in employer-employee disputes, if both sides listened (to the degree that they could simply repeat what the other side said), conflicts would be settled 50% faster.

Increasing awareness. Think about all the people who cross your path every day. By adopting the Buddhist approach of "looking for the human in everything," you'll become more aware of the many individuals who touch your life, and grow in appreciation for those you come in contact with even fleetingly.

Expand your reach. The oral historian Studs Terkel famously spoke to people on the bus during his daily commute. He embraced the mantra, "Don't be an examiner, be the interested inquirer." Practice being curious, and more of your interactions will lead you to be empathetic.

Tell me more

Asking questions is connected to all these empathetic techniques. It's a skill that's often overlooked, but can be learned.

In order to ask good questions, we need to know how the other person is feeling. Empathizing goes beyond a mere statement of the facts (*Sorry about your dead dog*) to something more sensitive and nuanced (*I'm so sorry to hear about the death of your pet. What was she like?).*

We often observe others who are sad, angry, frustrated, and upset. If you want to empathize, the most effective way to do so is to ask questions to discover why they feel the way they do.

We've already discussed the reasons why we don't ask many questions. They include our desire to show how smart we are, and our inclination to impress others with our skill and knowledge.

Underlying these explanations is a lack of empathy. If you are empathy challenged, you may have no interest in the feelings of others. Maybe you think you have nothing to learn, or fear being bored.

Asking appropriate follow-up questions are particularly impactful. They "signal to your conversation partner that you are listening, care, and want to know more. People interacting with a partner who asks lots of follow-up questions tend to feel respected and heard."

These findings were validated in a 1997 study by psychologist Arthur Aron. He wanted to know whether two strangers could form a close relationship by having each of them ask the other 36 questions.

The questions started out broad and general and increased gradually in intensity. A control group was instructed to simply interact the way they normally would.

The pairs that asked questions in the assigned order reported a sense of immediate closeness similar to what more typically occurs over more extended time. Asking these questions resulted in a deeper empathetic connection than was experienced in the control group.

All they had to do was ask.

What's the Point?

A heightened sense of empathy will improve your relationships.

Be patient toward all that is unsolved in your heart and try to love the questions themselves, like locked rooms and like books that are now written in a very foreign tongue.
–Rainer Maria Rilke

Chapter Eleven

What to Ask?

There's a reason this book is titled *Ask*.

- If you want to make a connection with anyone, in any context, ask questions.

- If you want to fully engage others with 100 percent certainty, ask questions.

- If you want to be perceived as a better employee or as a better leader, ask questions.

- If you want to reap the benefits of being more empathetic, ask questions.

- If you want to deepen your relationships with everyone in your life, ask questions.

- If you want to be liked, ask questions.

The importance of asking questions – in lieu of conveying information – can't be overstated.

Let's look at the research on what I call "a question deficit" and *how* to ask questions in a way that will have the most positive impact.

A question deficit

In an article in the *Harvard Business Review*, Alison Wood Brooks and Leslie K. John explain the power of asking questions and how most of us come up short in this regard. As they observe, "Among the most common complaints people make after having a conversation, such as an interview, a first date, or a work meeting, is 'I can't believe [s/he] didn't ask me any questions.'"

You can learn a lot about the power of asking questions from an even seemingly superficial activity like speed dating. In their book, *Honest Signals: How They Shape Our World*, Alex Pentland and Tracy Heibeck looked at the dynamics of speed dating. Participants sit across a table from one another. They spend a few minutes chatting, and then move on to the next table. At the end of the encounter, each person secretly indicates whether they want to exchange phone numbers. If both parties consent, the organizers of the event will share their contact information.

Women consent to an exchange of phone numbers far less frequently than men. Men often experience the sting of rejection. To counter those feelings, researchers began coaching men to look for certain "honest signals" subconsciously conveyed by the women indicating a mutual regard. The goal was to better align the instances they would both consent to exchanging their phone numbers (thereby reducing the number of rejections). After being taught to look for signs of engagement, the men were able to determine with a high degree of accuracy whether the women they met would be receptive.

The researchers told the men to pay attention to two factors: high activity and low consistency.

"High activity" refers to animated facial expressions, head nodding and gesturing. The more active the woman appeared, the more likely she was to be genuinely interested.

"Low consistency" refers to a person's variability in tone. A monotone would likely indicate a lack of interest. High variability in tone might indicate interest and engagement.

There was an interesting by-product of the research – a disarmingly simple way to engage someone and get them to want your phone number – ask them questions. Asking questions triggers a positive response to the questioner.

All questions aren't created equal

People are understandably skeptical when I tell them the key to deepening relationships is asking open-ended questions, without trying to steer the conversation, to offer nothing declarative (unless asked), and to expect little reciprocity. They think it's either a gimmick or that they will be perceived as insincere. Yet, when done properly, most people aren't aware of how many questions they're being asked, and don't make the connection between question asking and liking.

As a questioner you'll be acutely aware you're doing something different, and it's having a powerful impact. Others won't be. They will be too busy answering your questions – if they are good ones.

You might think asking questions would be simple. It isn't. I learned this lesson the hard way.

When I started coaching investment advisors, I wasn't specific enough about what I meant when I would encourage them to "ask questions" rather than lecture or educate prospects and clients. Initially, I received negative feedback from those who "tried" my process. Advisors would tell me: *I asked questions just like you suggested and still didn't get the business.*

I asked them to give me examples. Here are typical questions they asked:

- *What are your specific retirement goals?*

- *What keeps you up at night?*

- *How much money do you have to invest?*

- *What are your yearly expenses?*

These are questions, but they aren't the right ones.

Let's assume you're going out on a first date. You meet for dinner. You immediately ask the other person these questions:

- *When in a relationship do you think it is appropriate to meet other family members?*

- *How soon are you interested in getting married if you meet the right person?*

- *How do you feel about having children?*

These are also questions, but they are presumptuous and off-putting, just like the questions my advisor clients asked prospects who were complete strangers. They are probing without having established a foundation of trust. These questions would likely be seen as aggressive instead of gentle.

These questions also suffer from being agenda-laden. While framed as questions, they are really statements conveying the orientation of the questioner. They are likely to make the listener feel like they're being put on the spot when they aren't ready to share personal information.

Not all questions have this effect. Good questions, properly framed, can deepen a connection, not thwart it.

I counseled my clients to take a different approach. I told them to think of the conversation as a chalkboard on which anything could be written. Their goal was to get the other person to fill it with their words. The best way to do this was to ask open-ended questions, with no agenda in mind.

I told them not to direct the conversation towards subjects they wanted to discuss, or even to try and make a point. Instead, they were just to view this first meeting as an opportunity to listen.

I encouraged them to show genuine curiosity by asking questions like: *How did you get to where you are today?* I advised them to analogize the conversation to their first date. The goal is simply to get to know the other person, to explore whether they have anything in common, and to decide whether it makes sense to pursue a relationship.

Those who made these changes saw their conversion rates soar.

Question-typing

There are different types of questions.

Introductory questions. When you initially meet someone, to break the ice, one party might ask perfunctory questions like: *How are you? Really warm today, isn't it?* These are valuable questions for breaking the ice, but they aren't the kind of questions that deepen a connection.

It's important to move on from these questions, but do so naturally, not artificially. Remember that it only takes one meaningful question to start the process of improving your relationship, so don't rush it. Make sure you are giving the other person time to "warm-up."

The Ask Pivot

If you're asked a question, consider turning it around and question the questioner. Briefly respond and then ask a related question by performing what I call the *Ask Pivot*.

If the other person says: *Is it always this warm here?* you can respond by saying: *Where are you from? What's the weather like there?* The goal is to empower the other person to speak and for you to listen.

When asked a question, it's not surprising to think it's your turn to talk. But when you implement the *Ask Pivot*, you turn the conversation over to the other person as quickly as possible.

When you're in pivot mode, talking is like holding a hot coal. The longer you talk, the more it burns. The easiest way to drop the coal is to answer briefly and then ask another question.

The *Ask Pivot* is extremely powerful. It works because people want to talk – especially about themselves. It makes them feel good and important, which is exactly how you want them to feel. And they've already tipped you off to a topic they are comfortable talking about by asking you a question. It's practically an invitation to ask them a similar question.

Full-switch questions. You respond and change the subject. In response to an inquiry about the weather, you might say: *Yes, it's unusually warm. Do you often attend these networking events?*

Often in these scenarios you'll be tempted to fill the conversational void with your own words instead of asking a question. *Don't do it.* Authentic relationships start by setting aside your agenda, concerns, and advice, and letting the other person share what's on their mind.

By asking a full-switch question, you're not attempting to control the conversation beyond making it not about you. Instead, when you change the topic, you signal you're interested in their opinion, and the neural pathways of their brain will be flooded with "happiness" hormones.

Follow-up questions. If someone tells you they are planning a trip to France, an initial follow-up question might be: *What cities will you be visiting? Will you get to see the countryside?* Asking follow-up questions can have a powerful impact in deepening relationships. Why? Because so few people ask them.

Ask yourself this question. When was the last time someone asked you a series of thoughtful follow-up questions when you said something you felt was really interesting? Most people have trouble recalling a single instance.

When you acknowledge what the other person has just said, you accept their feelings, and signal they have been heard. What better way to set the stage for trust than to ask a question that explores what was just said in an agenda-free manner – one that doesn't dictate the type of response expected?

Over the course of a single conversation I like to practice asking different types of questions. Sometimes, when I fly, my seat partner will ask an introductory question, and I'll do the same. After some initial chitchat, I'll use full-switch questions to change the topic and get them talking.

If my fellow passenger asks me what I do, I'll say I'm an author, and before they can ask another question, I'll implement the *Ask Pivot* to find out what they do. I'll then use my skill as an active listener to ask follow-up questions based on their answer (*What made you become a mechanical engineer? What kind of work do you do as a mechanical engineer? What do you find most gratifying about your work?*).

Often, they will still be talking when we pull up to the gate. Invariably, they thank me for the "conversation" as they hand me their card and ask that we "stay in touch."

Open closed questions

Hal Gregerson, author of *Questions Are the Answer,* believes that questions are the most productive "when they are open versus closed, short versus long, and simple versus complex." There is ample support for this view. Those responding are likely to provide more complete answers, sometimes revealing feelings they might not disclose in response to narrower questions. These questions also reveal your "humility," as well as your willingness to learn.

As Edgar Schein of MIT describes them, they involve "the fine art of drawing someone out, of asking questions to which you do not already know the answer, of building a relationship based on curiosity and interest in the other person."

Open-ended questions generally begin with *who, what, when, where* and *why*. Here are some examples of how to start an open-ended question:

- *What was it like to…*

- *What was the best part of…*

- *What was the hardest part about…*

- *How did you feel about…*

- *How did you know…*

- *What brought you to…*

- *What's surprised you the most about…*

- *In what way is that similar/different from…*

- *Why do you want…*

We don't have to guess at the kinds of questions that will help us make deeper connections in a social context. Recall the study by psychologist Arthur Aron. He asked participants to pose predetermined open-ended questions in their interactions with strangers. When they did, they developed a sense of closeness very quickly. These questions aren't limited to meetings with strangers. They can be used to deepen the connections you have with others in your life. Note the specificity – yet the open-endedness– of just a couple of them:

- *If you could change anything about the way you were raised, what would it be?*

- *What is your most treasured memory?*

- *If your house caught on fire, and you had time to safely make a final dash to save any one item in it, what would it be? Why?*

Questions like these are representative of the type of inquiry that makes a powerful impact.

Another way to think about these questions is through an exercise where you "pop" open a closed question. *Did that work for you?* which can be answered with a simple *yes* or *no* turns into *What do you think about that?* Asking, *Have you done that before?* turns into *What happened when you did this before?* And, *Do you like this?* turns into, *What would you most want to change about…?*

A hidden peril

What all these questions have in common is an inability to anticipate what the other person is going to say. While being empathetic requires us to put ourselves in the shoes of the other person, few understand this can be very difficult, largely because we make so many erroneous assumptions.

This was pointedly brought to my attention in my marriage. My wife spends months on a single painting. She returned home one night and told me she threw her most recent painting out and was going to start again. As someone trained to empathize, I wanted to put myself in her shoes and experience the pain I assumed she was feeling. I offered what I thought was the perfect empathetic response: *That must be so frustrating for you.*

It wasn't. I made a common error. Instead of understanding what *she* was feeling, I *assumed* her feelings were the same as mine would be in her situation. I unwittingly substituted my way of thinking for her perspective because I thought I knew her well enough to understand her feelings.

Her reply spoke volumes: *Not at all. It was actually liberating. I learned a lot. It will be easier for me to start all over again.*

Accurately experiencing the feelings of others is exceedingly difficult. I'm not an artist. I don't understand the process artists engage in to create a painting that meets their standards.

There are many other situations where my perspective would likely be incorrect. I've never lived in poverty, been homeless, or been in prison. My assumptions about what it would be like to be in these situations – and my ability to ask the right questions or otherwise respond appropriately – would likely be wrong-headed despite my best intentions.

There's a simple way to avoid these misunderstandings and ask suitable, empathetic questions: ask.

Nicholas Epley, one of the co-authors of a study on the difference between perspective taking and perspective getting, offered an example which involved his wife, who often expressed her love for dolphins. As a Christmas present, he gave her a day with an animal handler at an aquarium. It was a perfect gift – except it wasn't.

She had recently given birth and "was in no mood to squeeze into a wet suit and hold stinky fish while exhausted from lack of sleep." Instead of "taking" his wife's perspective (which involved a series of flawed assumptions), here's what he should have done: ask her first. If he had, he would have given her what she desperately wanted: the opportunity to take a nap.

As Epley explains, "The secret to understanding each other better seems to come not through an increased ability to read body language or improved perspective taking but rather through the hard relational work of putting people in a position where they can tell you their minds openly and honestly."

All you need to do is ask compassionate open-ended questions.

Work at asking questions

The workplace is fertile ground for asking questions, but we often make problems worse by succumbing to our inclination to make incorrect assumptions and offer unsolicited advice.

Imagine you know someone who is going through a divorce and is having difficulty coping at work. You could assume they didn't initiate the divorce, but would that be right? You could assume they are worried about money or their living arrangements, but would that be right? You could even speculate they might think they will never find love again – but that would also be a guess.

Instead of starting from how *you* might feel if you were going through a divorce, consider asking an empathetic question like: *What can I do to help you through this difficult time?*

Questions like this one seem intuitive, but often they're not. If the co-worker is also going through a divorce, it's tempting to shift the conversation to their experience, in the mistaken belief that sharing similar experiences is helpful.

Their reality might be quite different from your perception. Maybe they're elated at the prospect of getting a divorce and are having trouble concentrating at work because they're so excited about starting over.

What's the Point?

Asking the right questions requires you
to avoid making assumptions.

When we talk about emotion, we really talk about
a collection of behaviors that are produced by the brain.
– Antonio Damasio

Chapter Twelve

What If You Had No Feelings?

I t's likely the vast majority of your conversations have a goal, like closing a sale or achieving consensus on a decision, or telling your child what to do. *Ask* recalibrates the conversation measuring stick. Your new goal is to forge an emotional connection.

The role emotions play in the way we function explains why *Ask* is so effective.

Facts have no feelings

Have you ever watched two people debate climate change? Those who believe in climate change discuss the scientific evidence relating to carbon dioxide, greenhouse gases and climate modeling. They buttress their data by referencing the scientific consensus on these issues. Often, their presentations lack an emotional connection.

Those who don't believe in climate change often elevate emotion over facts. They ask questions like: *If there is climate change, why was it so cold in Chicago today?* They share their fears about massive unemployment potentially caused by regulations intended to deal with climate change. And they make additional claims rooted in feelings like: *Al Gore was just trying to get elected*, and *climate scientists are in it for the money.*

Both sides are talking past each other, with the believers emphasizing facts and the deniers elevating emotions over facts that support their view.

The simple truth is that facts don't speak to emotions. Skeptics will process the information, but without an emotional connection, it won't change their minds. Advocates for climate change need to give doubters more than data.

What if climate change advocates talked about the higher incidence of illness, emergency room visits and deaths being caused now by climate change? Or the fact that extreme heat kills more Americans each year, on average, than hurricanes, tornadoes, floods, and lightning combined?

These are facts, but they're connected to powerful emotions. Taking it a step further, what if they used the data to personalize climate change, and pushed emotions to the forefront of the discussion. Anthony Leiserowitz, head of the Yale Project on Climate Change Communication, puts it this way: "One message that works across all groups is the health message: It's not just about polar bears and plants and penguins, it's about people."

It's not surprising that psychological researchers found emotions are the most effective method for communicating the risks of climate change.

When there's a debate where one side relies primarily on facts, and the other puts emotion at the forefront, the emotional argument is likely to prevail. Understanding why is key for shifting our understanding about the goals of communication.

The hierarchy of emotions

Think of the brain as a giant funnel. Every minute of your waking day, you are confronted with all kinds of information. You hear sounds, smell odors, touch things, see objects, talk with other people, and make thousands of judgments. The aggregate amount of data your brain is coping with could be as much as ten trillion bits per second. Your brain needs to prioritize, or it will be overwhelmed.

The brain gives information a well-defined pecking order. At the top is information that signals possible danger. Fear is a great motivator. It doesn't have to take the form of being physically attacked. It's generally accepted among behavioral economists that losses hurt more than gains. People don't want to lose more than they want to win.

Other emotions follow right behind. If you feel that one choice is better (or less risky) than another, you're more likely to choose it – even if logically it makes no sense.

Most people don't blink at the thought of getting a CT scan, but blanch at the risk of living near a nuclear power plant – even though there's little to support the concern that U.S. nuclear power plants adversely affect public health and safety.

Factual data is at the bottom of the brain's pecking order. It responds slowly when required to integrate facts, compare them with past experiences, and interpret them in a rational manner. In fact, psychologists have divided the decision-making systems of the brain into two: the fast emotional system of decision-making, and a slower rational process.

Your brain not only processes emotional and factual data differently, it also stores them in separate areas of the brain.

Facts you don't feel strongly about, such as what you had for dinner last night, are stored in the front and temporal cortexes. Events that triggered an emotional reaction, such as a marriage proposal or a breakup, are initially kept accessible in the hippocampus. That's because the brain "likes" emotional information (both positive and negative).

According to psychological researchers, that's why emotional memories are so vivid. The victim of a traumatic attack can relive all of the horrific details by revisiting the scene of the crime, even many years later. Negative events (death of a loved one or a terrible accident) particularly resonate. Your brain stores – and instantly recalls – these powerful emotional experiences. According to psychologist Elke Weber, if we feared climate change, we'd do more about it.

The same level of recall occurs with positive emotional events like the birth of a child, a special trip, or graduation. That explains why you can forget where you put your glasses ten minutes ago, but vividly recall your high school prom.

What's called "emotional memory enhancement" has been demonstrated to be much more powerful than trying to rationally figure out where you last had your car keys. As one researcher noted, "Emotional content is remembered more accurately and/or more quickly than non-emotional content for both short and longer-term recall of visual images."

Unlike other brain functions, the ability to recall memories that are emotionally "tagged" does not appear to decline with age. Emotional connections can even survive significant impairments to the brain. A study in Japan found stories with a strong emotional content actually enhanced memory in patients with Alzheimer's.

A surprising cause of dysfunctionality

What if your brain is impaired and can't process emotions? Would that allow the rational parts of your brain to take over and make you "perfectly" rational, like Spock from Star Trek?

Neuroscientist Antonio Damasio is a leading researcher on the importance of emotions. He believes emotions are critical to virtually every decision. Think about ordering at your favorite restaurant. You don't objectively evaluate every item on the menu, calculating calories and nutritional value. Instead, you remember having a particular dish that you really enjoyed. The memory of that positive experience will likely drive your choice.

In his book, *Descartes' Error*, Damasio reports on the results of experiments where he compared those who suffered serious brain trauma with those whose brains were normal. He found brain injuries that impaired the ability to experience emotion significantly impacted the ability to make decisions.

He described a patient he named "Elliot" who required the removal of a brain tumor from his frontal lobe. Elliot's ability to process information was left intact. He was "coherent and smart," able to discuss political affairs, and had a "flawless memory for his life story."

Yet the operation left Elliot with a major deficit: he was unable to experience emotion. When he was shown emotionally charged images (burning buildings, terrible accidents, people who were drowning), his reaction was indifferent. They stirred up no emotion (positive or negative).

Prior to the operation, he had a good job and a happy marriage. He was considered a model for his younger siblings and colleagues. After the operation he couldn't hold down a job, got a divorce, and even bankrupted himself by getting involved in a shady pyramid scheme. Why did a perfectly rational man come undone?

Researchers point the finger at Elliot's inability to experience emotion and how it impacted his ability to make decisions. He could "rationally" assess the merit of whether to buy or sell a stock or choose among different dinner options, but couldn't "emotionally" pull the trigger. He obsessed over how to perform basic tasks, apparently paralyzed by his choices.

According to Damasio, "The cold-bloodedness of Elliot's reasoning prevented him from assigning different values to different options."

Emotions don't get in the way of decisions. Just the opposite. Without emotions we cannot make decisions at all.

Damasio's view of the importance of emotions in decision-making is shared by psychologists who "now assume that emotions are the dominant driver in most decisions in life." It's not surprising they play such a critical role in relationships.

Like a car without an engine

It's impossible to forge a positive relationship without making an emotional connection. The best way to make that happen is by asking empathetic, thoughtful and sincere questions and appropriate follow-up questions. This is the essence of *Ask*.

If your goal is to make an emotional connection with someone of another gender, understand there are fundamental differences in how men and women communicate. In his book,

Brain Rules, developmental molecular biologist John Medina explains that women tend to recall "emotional biographical events" (a vacation, a first date) more vividly than men. Women also are generally better at communicating than men when emotions are involved.

Deborah Tannen, author of *You Just Don't Understand: Women and Men in Conversation*, gives this example of this difference. Three boys were talking about Disneyland. One indicates his family stayed three days. The second boy responded that they stayed four days. The third boy said, "We are going to move to Disneyland", which was untrue. Each boy competed to one-up the other.

In contrast, Tannen relates this story about two little girls who were talking about siblings. One said she had a brother named Benjamin and another one named Jonathan. The other girl responded by saying she had brothers with the same names, when, in fact, she didn't.

Tannen explained: "She was simply offering a matching experience as a sign of goodwill, to reinforce the friendship."

The focus of males on dominance and females on feelings can create barriers to making an emotional connection.

In the adult world these differences can lead to very different – and discriminatory – perceptions of similar behavior by men and women. An assertive woman can be characterized as "bossy and aggressive." The same conduct by a man may be praised as "decisive and assertive."

Understanding these differences can help make for better relationships if the knowledge is used to *support* the emotional needs of the other person.

You don't have to worry about shying away from hard conversations. There's lots of research suggesting that engaging in talk about emotions leads to positive outcomes, even if the talk is about negative emotions.

It doesn't matter if the relationship is new or old – talk about emotions heightens intimacy. The research revealed that this carried over to relationships on social media. Facebook users who talk more about their emotions actually have more and deeper friendships than those who do not.

Regardless of gender, if you are looking for an emotional connection, you're not going to find it if you talk louder, lecture, interrupt, and dominate the conversation. A more effective strategy would be to make inquiries that will elicit the other person's views. Repeat back what they say so they know you understood them. Don't interrupt, even if you feel compelled to do so.

It's contagious

An "emotional" conversation won't bring two people closer if they are shouting epithets at each other. There's a big difference between being emotional and talking about your emotions. Being emotional isn't a particularly good state to be in because of what's known as "emotional contagion." Our emotions can spread to others, even unintentionally.

One study examined the moods of 65 community nurses in three teams, and 9 accountants and their colleagues. It found employees adopted the same emotional state as the collective mood of their teammates, regardless of whether the emotional state was positive or negative. When this contagion occurs, the people involved generally are not aware of it.

There's clear evidence positive emotions (like joy, gratitude, confidence, happiness and optimism) "bring people together" and "almost seem necessary for forming and maintaining relationships." These emotions foster "more enjoyable social interactions" and "greater friendship closeness."

In romantic relationships, there's support for the view that feeling connected to your partner in a positive way correlated with the depth and sustainability of the relationship.

In one experiment, researchers showed pairs of circles marked "self" and "other" to thousands of couples. The circle pairs ranged from not overlapping at all, to almost complete overlapping. Couples were asked to choose the pair that most accurately represented how connected they felt to their partner.

The quality and sustainability of their relationship was directly related to how much of an overlap there was in the pair of circles they chose. Couples who were the most committed to the relationship were more motivated to maintain it. Those couples felt a deep psychological attachment to each other.

In her book, *The Influential Mind*, Tali Sharot describes a process she calls "coupling." She describes it as a feeling that you "click with another person...when complete comprehension emerges between two communicating individuals. This occurs when the two brains "synchronize."

When we hear (from loved ones, friends or even strangers) stories laden with emotion, our brains not only feel connected to theirs, but we may even anticipate what they are about to say. Sharot calls this an enhanced level of emotional connection that "promotes social interaction."

I call it having a meaningful relationship.

What you don't say has an impact

How can you can convey positive emotions? Obviously asking questions in a compassionate, empathetic fashion is crucial. But it's not just what you say. It's *how* you say it that also matters.

One study examined the relationship between the voice tone of surgeons during routine office visits, and their history of being sued for malpractice. Their voice tone was rated for warmth, hostility, dominance and anxiety from 10-second voice recordings. The study found surgeons whose voice tone was rated highly for warmth and caring had fewer malpractice claims.

"Likeability" also affected these results. The surgeons who were warm and caring were perceived as more likeable. A malpractice attorney who represents injured patients had this sage observation: "In all the years I've been in this business, I've never had a potential client walk in and say, 'I really like this doctor, and I feel terrible about doing it, but I want to sue him.'" Physicians who strike a personal note with their patients, spending time with them, asking questions and providing useful information about their course of treatment while exhibiting a sense of humor and coming across as relatable, were much less likely to be sued.

If you don't think this applies to personal relationships, consider the high percentage of marriages that end with one partner suing the other for divorce.

According to David Hoffeld, author of *The Science of Selling*, your non-verbal behavior (folding your arms, leaning forward or backward, clenching your fist, your facial expression) can impact both your emotional state and the emotional state of the other person.

The most basic yet compelling example is the act of smiling. It can make you feel "more optimistic, energetic, and productive." Smiling also increases blood flow to the brain, producing pleasurable feelings and putting you in a better mood. These positive changes are not limited to your emotional state. They will be "caught" by the other person as well.

That's important. Researchers have argued that while verbal factors are important, nonverbal behaviors play a critical role in creating and sustaining intimate interactions and relationships. That's because nonverbal communication sets the stage for intimacy.

No one will want to answer your questions, no matter how open-ended they are, if your body language says, "I'm not interested."

What's the Point?

Don't underestimate the role of emotions or overestimate the role of facts in your relationships.

•Part Five•

The Payoff is Worth The Challenge

Can you learn to ask in the most difficult circumstances?

*The brain is like Velcro for negative experiences,
but Teflon for positive ones.*
– Rick Hanson, Ph.D.

Chapter Thirteen

Can You Overcome the Negative?

I magine being a car salesperson. You have a track record of being a top producer, but the last month has been particularly slow. You feel like a failure. You're concerned you could be fired and not be able to find another job. You think about losing your home.

You're experiencing negativity bias, causing you to lose perspective and focus on the most adverse consequences.

Everyone does it, including myself. When I was a trial lawyer, I won some cases, but also lost my fair share. That's unremarkable. No one prevails in every trial. However, my reaction to winning and losing was markedly different.

I was happy when I won, but that feeling was fleeting. I quickly put the victory out of my mind and moved on to the next case.

When I lost, I would obsessively ruminate. I questioned everything, especially my competence.

A centrifugal pull...in the wrong direction

I didn't realize it, but I was experiencing the powerful impact of negativity bias.

We're inclined to pay more attention to negatives than positives. Negatives linger far longer. We fear a trip to the dentist more as it gets closer than we enjoy the thought of a Caribbean vacation as it approaches.

When we tally the pros and cons about a job change or a move, we give more weight to the negatives than the positives. We even mentally picture negatives as more vivid and more varied than positives. It's why the sensation of defeat lingers, while the pleasures of success are fleeting.

Professor Roy Baumeister summed up this point of view in his pointedly titled paper, "Bad is Stronger than Good." He catalogued the numerous ways negativity bias can affect our personal relationships: traumatic events can drive a wedge between a couple instead of drawing them closer. Negative stereotypes of the other gender can undermine their positive attributes.

Negativity bias can undercut our best intentions when implementing *Ask*. If the person we are focused on says something negative, it's going to hurt. Worse, negativity bias is reciprocal: we are likely going to respond negatively as well. It turns into a cascade of negativity. It's almost impossible to authentically engage with others when you're busy "defending" yourself.

Asking the right questions will redirect your focus away from a negative comment to the deeper bonds you are forging by staying positive. Those connections set the stage for a long-term productive relationship.

It's in your DNA

Our proclivity to overreact to negative events is well-documented. We are hard-wired to give precedence to negative events.

The different reaction of our brain to positive and negative events was demonstrated in a study from The Ohio State University. The authors showed participants images likely to generate neutral reactions (a plate, a hair dryer, an electrical outlet), positive responses (red Ferrari, people enjoying a roller coaster) as well as negative ones (a mutilated face, handgun aimed at the camera).

While the participants were viewing the images, one of the authors of the study recorded the electrical activity in their cerebral cortex (which engages in information processing). He found there was a greater surge in electrical neural activity when negative images were shown.

Setting aside the damage negativity bias does to our relationships, psychologist Suzanne Segerstrom found that ten years after graduation, law students who were more generally optimistic earned an average of $32,667 more than their negatively oriented peers.

That's a lot of cash to leave on the table by being negative.

Negatives dominate

Researchers theorize negative events are more complex than positive ones. It's much less challenging to choose between two different flavors of ice cream than it is to assess potential negative outcomes.

Is the threat real? Do you run or ignore it? What are your chances if you stay and fight? Strawberry or chocolate? That last question is not remotely the same kind of stressor as the first three. The need to consider threatening alternatives causes our brains to prioritize negative emotions over pleasurable ones. Negative events have more "negative potential," meaning even minimal exposure can cause maximum damage. Negative thoughts are not unlike germs. Both are self-replicating, and even minor contact can cause an "infection."

Pervasive impact

While it's true that positive and negative emotions are both contagious, the impact of negative emotions is far more pervasive. When we're filled with negativity, those feelings are likely to quickly impact those around us, with the potential to have tremendously negative effects in the workplace, and even create a "culture of negativity."

Negativity bias in personal relationships can be especially pernicious because it causes us to focus on the one time your partner did something wrong and overlook the many things they did right. It appears our memory of past negative actions primes us to anticipate future negativity, even if most of our interactions are positive.

Add to this the fact that men and women often deal differently with negativity bias and you have a potentially volatile situation. Women will tend to avoid negativity, or otherwise internalize their feelings, resulting in sadness or even depression. Men may externalize these feelings, eager to confront the negativity head on by expressing anger or other hostile emotions.

Making a relationship last is easier if you can cope with – and even reverse – some of the effects of negativity bias.

Negativity hacks

It's not easy to find a work-around for what's been hard-wired into your brain over thousands of years. Thankfully, some of this happens naturally.

As we age, we process events less negatively and attach less negative emotion to them. We are less likely to remember events as negative. While it doesn't appear that we naturally become more positive as we age, our reaction to negativity appears to decline as we age.

How do we "speed up" the natural processes for becoming less negative, while learning to bring positive thinking to the forefront? One way to get a handle on your emotions and tune into your positive emotional state is simply to name them.

When you recognize you're sliding into negativity bias, try to understand what's happening. If you can label it, it's a short step to giving yourself a bit of a reality check: *I know what I'm doing. I'm focusing on the negatives and not considering the positives.* As the clinical psychologist Elisha Goldstein notes, "The moment we name it, we can approach it and work with it."

Negativity bias can make us fearful, suspicious and jaded. These feelings are often the product of incorrect *assumptions*. Ask yourself questions like: *Why am I feeling this way? Am I being objective or succumbing to negativity?*

Then turn those questions around and direct them at the person you think you might be making assumptions about. When you are with someone and feel like negativity bias is creeping into your interactions, ask questions.

This one is my favorite for those close to me: *Is there anything unspoken between us?*

If a particular situation causes anxiety, ask questions to deal with it, rather than making assumptions and accusations. Falsely accusing someone of infidelity is much different from simply asking, *Would you be willing to text me the next time you are going to be more than thirty minutes late?*

After asking your questions, it's time to engage in some relationship rebuilding. Research on couples done by Dr. John Gottman and Robert Levenson dealt with the importance of positive emotions in building healthy relationships. They taped participants trying to resolve a conflict in their relationship for 15 minutes and studied them closely, then predicted which couples would stay together and which would divorce. They followed up with the participants nine years later, and discovered their predictions were 90% accurate.

What was their secret? All they did was count the positive and negative interactions during the argument, and then predicted a "breaking point." What's telling is that they settled on the ratio of 5 to1 as the inflection point – for every negative interaction, couples who stayed together had a minimum of 5 positive ones. It wasn't just that their partners showered them with insincere compliments either – genuine interactions were key.

If you want to have a stable, fulfilling relationship, be on high alert for negative behavior, like being overly critical or dismissive, showing contempt, and eye-rolling. Instead, orient yourself towards a complimentary, curious attitude towards your partner.

A great opening

My wife and I have a pact. Whoever initiates a discussion that could lead to a criticism has to start by saying, "I love you very much …." By doing this, we jump start the positive/negative ratio found by Gottman and Levenson. Here are some other examples of positive interactions they found:

Listening. When couples argue, they don't really listen. They talk over each other, interrupt or use body language (like folded arms) indicating they are not really "listening." You can't listen when you are really just waiting for the other person to stop talking so you can make your point.

Affection. It's easy to lose perspective when you are arguing. Is "winning" the argument really more important than compromising your relationship? Gottman and Levenson make this observation: "If you're having a difficult conversation and your partner takes your hand and says, 'Gosh, this is hard to talk about. I really love you and I know we can figure this out together,' you will likely feel better because their display of affection is bound to reduce tension and bring you closer together."

Goodwill. In a healthy relationship, both parties build up "equity" through consistent conduct showing thoughtfulness and consideration, much like paying a mortgage every month. This "equity" shouldn't get eliminated by an isolated act that triggers an argument.

That's why I hold the unpopular view that special "days" (like Mother's Day and Father's Day) turn reality on its head. If you really love your Mom, Dad, spouse or partner, every day should be "their" day. If you want to invest some sweat equity in your relationship, start making deposits in the emotional piggy bank by asking questions.

Search for agreement. Having an argument means you're having a disagreement. It doesn't mean you disagree about everything. Look for "alliances" – areas where you can agree, even if they are relatively minor.

Let's say you're arguing about allocation of household chores. One party believes there isn't an equal contribution. If you're the one being criticized, you could say: *So we agree that I do some of the chores, but just not enough of them, right?* Then continue to ask questions: *What if I agreed to do all the chores on the weekend, would that help resolve our issue?*

Especially in a conflict, flipping your brain from making declarative statements to asking questions changes the entire tenor of the discussion. It demonstrates you're interested – and value – the viewpoint of the other person, and that you're actively looking for a solution.

Apologize. We're not perfect. We make mistakes. We say things we wish we could retract. There's a saying that "words are like spent bullets. You can't take them back." We do things that can legitimately be interpreted as thoughtless even if unintentional. It's hard to admit your mistake and apologize. But an apology does wonders for forging a deeper, more honest, and ultimately more positive relationship. Do it sincerely and express empathy. Demonstrate you understand how the other person could feel hurt by saying: *I can see how you took what I said that way. I feel terrible about it.*

Validate. It's rare there aren't legitimate arguments on both sides of a disagreement. For example, if you want to go on a vacation with your spouse, and she wants to spend that time with her parents, there is no "right" or "wrong" answer. But validating her feelings is different from capitulating.

Telling your partner, *I know you haven't seen your parents in a while and you're really close to them, so I can understand why you want to spend time there,* is different from *agreeing* to do so. Having empathy for her view will change the dynamic of the argument and set the stage for compromise.

Avoid the "cardinal sin" of digging in and holding forth that yours is the only perspective worth listening to. A compromise might be to spend one week with your spouse's parents and another on vacation.

When you validate the legitimacy of another viewpoint, you turn a negative into a positive.

If the only time you express your feelings is during a conflict, the outcome isn't going to be pretty. It's easy to express love, gratitude and appreciation when things are going well.

How often do you say things like, *I'm so grateful to be married to you, I love you more every day,* and *I appreciate everything about you*?

If you fill your relationship with positive emotions, it will be well-fortified to withstand the negative ones that inevitably arise.

What's the Point?

Learn to recognize, name and
tame negativity bias.

Love is supposed to lift you up, not hold you down.
It is supposed to push you forward, not hold you back.
– Suzy Kassem

Chapter Fourteen

What's the Best Way to Turn Conflict into Collaboration?

It's not just our country that's polarized. Our relationships are as well. Whether it's the people closest to us, or our colleagues at work, nurturing and enriching relationships have been replaced by stress, tension and conflict.

Asking questions can have a transformational impact on the connections we have with others.

It's chemical

There are strategies for coping when tempers are heated and disagreements erupt. Implementing them requires some knowledge of what happens to the brain in highly stressful circumstances.

Being "attacked" comes in many forms. It can be physical but more typically is verbal. The source can be a loved one, a colleague at work, or even a stranger. Whatever the context, your brain (specifically your amygdala, which is the integrative center for emotions, emotional behavior and motivation) goes into overdrive. Adrenaline and cortisol flood our system. Our pulses race. We feel sweaty. The rate of our breathing changes.

According to Diane Hamilton, an expert on conflict resolution, these changes deprive us of our ability to evaluate multiple perspectives, cause us to become disoriented, and may even impair our memory – not exactly the prescription for successful interactions.

Conflict hacks

Hamilton has a number of suggestions for overcoming these obstacles. These include staying in the present, letting go of your agenda, and pivoting to more helpful ways of interacting.

Consider how these strategies help diffuse stressful situations and facilitate resolution:

Actively listen. If you let the other person speak without interruption and focus intensely on what they're saying (instead of formulating a defense), you're much more likely to get to the root of the issue. That's because active listening is an exercise in being empathetic – in this instance, with a person who feels so deeply misunderstood they are lashing out.

By actively listening and trying to understand their perspective without imposing your own interpretation on the events they are describing, you are *really* trying to understand their point of view.

This sort of unconditional willingness to listen in an unbiased and fair-minded way earns trust. You are more likely to find common ground, particularly if you repeat back a clear and coherent summary of what was said and how they feel. If you then ask specific follow up questions to indicate your interest in learning more, you demonstrate you are taking what they said seriously, and you're showing genuine concern.

Ask questions. Your questions should reflect what you heard. You should be asking for elaboration and clarification, and your questions should reflect a genuine and sincere interest in understanding the conflict. By insuring you're present and tuned into the other person, you guarantee your questions won't be perceived as canned or rote, which will immediately be recognized and undo all your good work.

Asking thoughtful follow-up questions, where you explore the other person's point of view, has a powerful impact in deepening relationships because it's so rare.

Acknowledging and validating the other person creates a framework of trust that can serve as the ground for resolving conflict. By listening to their responses in full, and not cutting them off to pursue your own agenda, you demonstrate they are heard.

Listening and validating their feelings is not the same thing as agreeing with their perspective. It's saying you don't believe that your point of view is the only one that matters.

Ending the argument. Once you fully understand the issue, you can use the trust you've created to seek a resolution. You may not come to a perfect agreement, but you have reduced the likelihood of having to settle for "agree to disagree," which leaves everything status quo (including the friction).

Listening closely to the other person may make you aware that you made some mistakes that contributed to the disagreement, even if unintentionally. Taking responsibility for your actions and apologizing is very disarming. It sets the stage for moving forward. Then look for common ground. It doesn't matter what you can agree about. You don't have to resolve all the points at once.

If you have a particularly troubled relationship – perhaps with your sibling or your teenager – embracing questions can change the entire dynamic of the relationship.

Consider how you would feel if you were asked: *What are your thoughts on resolving this issue?* And upon hearing your answer, you were then asked: *Can we agree that...?* based on what you'd said.

You'd be more than just pleasantly surprised. You'd feel genuinely heard. It's hard to stay angry with someone who is sincerely listening.

The sad state of "happy" marriages

There's a serious disconnect between the idealized view of marriage and the stark reality confronting most relationships today. Dana Adam Shapiro, the author of *You Can Be Right (or You Can Be Married): Looking for Love in the Age of Divorce,* estimates only 17 percent of couples are happy.

Vicki Larson, co-author of *The New I do, Reshaping Marriage for Skeptics, Realists and Rebels,* believes the statistics paint an even more dismal picture. She estimates forty percent of couples are so unhappy they're thinking about ending their relationship.

The divorce rate in the US validates this troubled status. A young couple marrying for the first time today has a lifetime divorce risk of 40%.

Staying together if you're unhappy is not a "solution" either. The consequences of living in a troubled marriage are significant. They include deterioration in physical and mental health for the couple, and "mental, physical, educational and social problems" for their children.

Couples in a troubled relationship have children who are more likely to exhibit problems at home and in school. The root of these troubles is a pattern of failing to maintain open lines of communication, and an increased propensity to argue.

The frequency of arguments in relationships is stunning. A study in the United Kingdom found the average British family had a least three disagreements a day, equating to 1,095 arguments a year, lasting for more than 91 hours in total. Almost 10% of the participants reported they were not currently speaking to their partners due to a recent argument.

A survey done in the U.S. found American couples, on average, argued 19 times per month, resulting in one partner spending on average 5.5 nights a month on the couch.

The topics couples argue about cover a wide range of subjects, including children, in-laws, religion, drinking, affection, sex, and even how to spend leisure time.

A survey by *Money Magazine* found 70% of married couples argued about money. Common financial issues included too much spending, lack of a budget, debt, savings, and planning for retirement.

Another hot button topic for couples with children was chores and responsibilities. When chores weren't an issue, 83% described their relationship as "very happy."

Breaking the logjam

Whether the issue is chores or money, couples often find themselves locked in intractable positions, causing them to repeat the same arguments, ripping at the fabric of their relationships, with no resolution in sight. They validate the truism that "insanity is doing the same thing over and over again and expecting different results."

Simply asking the right questions can break this logjam and put couples on the path to enriching their relationships, rather than destroying them.

Let's use arguments about money as an example. We know from studies on naïve realism that we perceive situations through the lens of our biases. Your background impacts the way you see yourself and your attitude towards money.

There's considerable evidence that those from privileged backgrounds believe they are entitled to their wealth (even when it's inherited). They view themselves as fundamentally exceptional and may also believe those less fortunate are genetically inferior.

If your background was not privileged, your attitude towards money is likely different. Maybe money was a source of conflict, or money was used to control your behavior. Perhaps money flowed freely at one point, but then it was limited. Regardless of the attitude you have towards money, it is likely rooted in your early experiences, making it a highly emotional issue.

If both partners had different early experiences with money, the possibility for conflict is greatly enhanced. Whether one person is "right" or "wrong" is irrelevant. No matter how strongly you believe you are "right," your confidence may be misplaced. We are all experts in knowing how we feel. If your partner feels aggrieved, there's a problem that needs to be solved.

Approach this tinderbox by formulating thoughtful questions designed to elicit feelings, demonstrate your acknowledgment of the issue, and your commitment to resolving it. Here are some suggestions:

- *I understand we spend too much money and aren't saving enough, so what steps do you think we can take to resolve this issue?*

- *What if we came up with a goal of saving a certain percentage of our income every month and made it a point to hold each other accountable?*

- *Should I consider looking for a better paying job?*

- *Should we consider retaining a financial planner to help us?*

- *Are there any expenses that come to mind where I can cut back?*

- *Are there any apps we could use that would help us track our expenses?*

- *Can we agree that our relationship is much, much more important than this or any other issue?*

These questions could turn a potential argument into a relationship-enhancing and problem-solving experience. It's the difference between opposing parties and their lawyers sitting on different sides of a conference table, and both of you sitting on the same side of the table, next to each other, making physical contact, and working collaboratively.

Switch your focus

Many married couples seeking therapy report that the underlying cause of their marital discord was "problematic communication and lack of emotional affection." It's no surprise that lack of communication has a very damaging impact on the health of relationships. While there's no guarantee improving communication will resolve fundamental relationship issues, poor communication has been shown time and again to be a key source of dissatisfaction within marriages.

Imagine a situation where one partner is returning home after attending a 3-day conference, while the other partner held down the home front by taking time off from work to care for the kids. The caregiver welcomes home the conference goer with a softball question: *How was the conference?*

At this time, the partner who traveled has a choice. They can discuss the details of the conference, what they learned while they were away, and maybe even relate humorous anecdotes about the people they met. Doing so has considerable benefits to the speaker from a neuroscience perspective.

Unfortunately, because it is so highly pleasurable to talk about yourself, it will also lead to self-reinforcing behavior. Like any other addiction, once you experience the dopamine "high," you'll want it to continue and will be reluctant to "cede the floor." You may even rationalize dominating the conversation (if you think about it at all) because your experience was "obviously" more interesting than your partner's.

Or you could respond by performing the *Ask* Pivot: *It was really great. I learned a lot. What did you and the children do while I was away?* You can then ask thoughtful follow-up questions based on your active listening:

- *Tell me more about...*

- *What was that experience like?*

- *Would you do it again?*

- *What worked and what didn't in my absence?*

- *Is there anything I could have done before I left that would have made your life easier?*

Talking about yourself will make you feel great. Empowering your partner to talk requires discipline to defer that gratification and reap a huge benefit later – better communication and a stronger, healthier, deeper connection, leading to a happier, more satisfying relationship.

On its merits the "right" choice is obvious. But it requires the equivalent of declining an addictive drug which you know will give you a pleasurable high. Maybe that's the real definition of "love."

What's the Point?

Conflict can be converted – like lemons into lemonade – to deepen and enhance your relationships.

Vision without action is merely a dream.
Action without vision just passes the time.
Vision with action can change the world.
– Joel A. Barker

Chapter Fifteen

Did You Learn to Ask?

S tart this journey by taking small steps. A good place to begin is at home with people you love. Then, try it with friends, colleagues and extended family. Show a genuine and sincere interest in their lives by actively listening. Ditch your agenda. Exhibit curiosity and sincerity in your questions and encourage them to elaborate.

Don't expect reciprocity. Visualize meeting someone for the first time and later summarizing the interaction like this: *I asked a ton of questions. We spent our entire time together talking about her. She is genuinely interesting and I learned a lot from our conversation. Although she didn't ask me questions, I wasn't surprised. When I'm talking, I don't want to stop either.*

That would be a very successful encounter.

Ask isn't a gimmick. It's based on sound research. It's been field tested by thousands of people like you. It's as powerful with friends and family as it is in business.

Let me leave you with this thought.

Think about the people in your life who show a genuine and sincere interest in you. How do you feel about them? I'll bet you regard them as very special and important.

Now picture all the people with whom you interact.

What if they were asked whether there was someone in their life who always asks thoughtful questions and follows up with requests to clarify? Who listens intently? Who doesn't give advice, but is always there for them? Who has no agenda other than learning more about them and caring about their well-being?

What if all those people raised their hand said that person was you?

What if you became *that person*?

Judge a man by his questions rather than his answers.
—Voltaire

Chapter Sixteen

What Do You Want to Ask?

H ere are the questions I get asked most frequently about *Ask*:

Q. When do I get to talk?

A. There will be many times when the other person is so engaged in speaking that your opportunity to talk will be limited or even non-existent. While this can be frustrating, the upside is your relationship with that person will be deep and meaningful. Over time, they may start to reciprocate by asking questions. Until that happens, consider it the price you pay to be thought of as a kind and insightful friend, colleague, spouse or partner.

Q .What if the other person isn't interested in answering questions, even those that empower them to speak about themselves?

A. This issue typically arises in a business context.

When you implement *Ask*, you aren't trying to impose anything on anyone, including pressuring them to answer questions (regardless of how nicely phrased). If someone is reluctant to answer questions, pivot to this question (or something similar): *What would you like to talk about?*

Your goal is to find out their agenda and address it, not to insist on a particular format or topic of conversation.

Q. If I started asking questions of my spouse or partner, they would say "Why are you asking me so many questions?" How do I deal with that?

A. In all likelihood, they won't, assuming you are asking appropriate questions that reflect a genuine interest and not "cross-examining" them.

Q. In a business conversation, what if the other person just talks about themself and I never get a chance to discuss my product or service?

A. In most situations, that won't happen. The other person is well aware of the reason the two of you are talking. If they have questions, at some point, they will ask them. When they do, you can be confident you are responding to an issue of concern, rather than assuming what you have to say is of interest to them.

In the unlikely event the conversation goes "nowhere," I like your chances of landing the business. From the perspective of the prospect, the time spent with you has been unique, meaningful and enjoyable. He or she will have very positive feelings about you. Those feelings are what often translate into business.

Q. What's the biggest misunderstanding we have about communicating with others?

A. That they are interested in what we have to say. Most of the time, they aren't really listening. Instead, they are formulating their response to what we are saying to advance their agenda.

Q. What are the most important things I can do right now?

A. Don't try to be the most interesting person in the room. Be the most *interested.*

Get in the habit of starting sentences with *I'm curious....*

Use these five words more frequently: *Tell me more about that.*

Retrain your brain to elicit information rather than convey it.

Remember, there is no more compelling evidence of kindness than empowering people to talk about themselves.

Q. *What if the other person has read Ask and we are competing for who can ask the most questions?*

A. The power of the principles in *Ask* are so potent the other person rarely wants to cede the floor. If you are fortunate enough to find someone who asks thoughtful questions, you will have a wonderful, mutually enjoyable conversation. It's unlikely to turn into a competition about who can ask the most questions.

Endnotes

Chapter 1

1. Tellegen et al., "Personality Similarity in Twins Reared Apart and Together," *Journal of Personality and Social Psychology* 54, no. 6 (June 1988): 1031–39, doi:10.1037//0022-3514.54.6.1031.

2. P. Brickman, D. Coates, and R. Janoff-Bulman, "Lottery Winners and Accident Victims: Is Happiness Relative?" *Journal of Personality and Social Psychology* 36, no. 8 (Sep 1978): 917–27, doi:10.1037//0022-3514.36.8.917.

3. David A. Schkade and Daniel Kahneman, "Does Living in California Make People Happy? A Focusing Illusion in Judgments of Life Satisfaction," *Psychological Science* 9, no. 5 (Sep 1998): 340–46. http://www.jstor.org/stable/40063318.

4. Jasper Bergink, "Happiness: It's Not Just Your Genes, Stupid!" *For A State of Happiness* (blog), September 17, 2015, http://www.forastateofhappiness.com/tag/50-10-40-formula/.

5. Sonja Lyubomirsky, Kennon M. Sheldon, and David Schkade, "Pursuing Happiness: The Architecture of Sustainable Change," *Review of General Psychology* 9, no. 2 (2005): 111–31, doi:10.1037/1089-2680.9.2.111.

6. Todd B. Kashdan, "What Really Makes You a Happy Person?" *Psychology Today*, August 19, 2015, https://www.psychologytoday.com/us/blog/curious/201508/what-really-makes-you-happy-person.

7. Bergink, "Happiness: It's Not Just Your Genes, Stupid!"

8. Lyubomirsky, Sheldon, and Schkade, "Pursuing Happiness: The Architecture of Sustainable Change."

9. Edward L. Deci and Richard M. Ryan, "The 'What' and 'Why' of Goal Pursuits: Human Needs and the Self-Determination of Behavior," *Psychological Inquiry* 11, no. 4 (Nov 2009): 227–68, doi:10.1207/S15327965PLI1104_01.

10. Kerry J. Stewart, "Physical Activity and Aging," *Annals of the New York Academy of Sciences* 1055, no. 1 (Jan 2006): 193–206, doi:10.1196/annals.1323.029.

11. Jennifer Weuve et al., "Physical Activity, Including Walking, and Cognitive Function in Older Women," *The Journal of the American Medical Association* 292, no. 12 (Sep 2004): 1454–61, doi:10.1001/jama.292.12.1454.

12. Suvi Rovio et al., "Leisure-Time Physical Activity at Midlife and the Risk of Dementia and Alzheimer's Disease," *The Lancet Neurology* 4, no. 11 (Nov 2005): 705–11, doi:10.1016/S1474-4422(05)70198-8.

13. L. Clarkson-Smith and A. A. Hartley, "Relationships between Physical Exercise and Cognitive Abilities in Older Adults," *Psychology and Aging* 4, no. 2 (June 1989): 183–89, doi:10.1037//0882-7974.4.2.183.

14. "Why Good Nutrition Is Important," Center for Science in the Public Interest, https://cspinet.org/eating-healthy/why-good-nutrition-important.

15. Lauren Gray, "50 Amazing Health Facts That Will Improve Your Health," BestLife, July 25, 2019, https://bestlifeonline.com/shocking-health-facts/.

16. "New Dietary Guidelines Urge Americans to Eat Less Added Sugars, Saturated Fat, and Sodium," National Heart, Lung, and Blood Institute, March 2, 2016, https://www.nhlbi.nih.gov/news/2016/new-dietary-guidelines-urge-americans-eat-less-added-sugars-saturated-fat-and-sodium.

17. "Chapter 2: Shifts Needed To Align With Healthy Eating Patterns," in *Dietary Guidelines for Americans 2015–2020*, 8th ed., Health.gov, accessed February 3, 2020, https://health.gov/dietaryguidelines/2015/guidelines/Chapter-2/a-closer-look-at-current-intakes-and-recommended-shifts/#other-components.

18. Mariana Pascha, "18 Heart-Warming Acts of Kindness That Will Make You Cry," PositivePsychology.com, June 19, 2019, https://positivepsychology.com/acts-of-kindness/.

19. Jane Lampman, "Researchers Say Giving Leads to a Healthier, Happier Life," The Christian Science Monitor, July 25, 2007, https://www.csmonitor.com/2007/0725/p13s02-lire.html.

20. Press Association, "Volunteering 'Boosts Community Happiness'" *The Guardian*, September 20, 2004, https://www.theguardian.com/society/2004/sep/20/research.highereducation.

21. Emiliana R. Simon-Thomas, "Three Insights from the Cutting Edge of Compassion Research," *Greater Good Magazine*, September 7, 2012, https://greatergood.berkeley.edu/article/item/three_insights_from_the_cutting_edge_of_compassion_research.

22. South West News Service, "Americans Check Their Phones 80 Times a Day: Study," *New York Post*, November 8, 2017, https://nypost.com/2017/11/08/americans-check-their-phones-80-times-a-day-study/.

23. Cheri D. Mah et al., "The Effects of Sleep Extension on the Athletic Performance of Collegiate Basketball Players," *Sleep Research Society* 34, no. 7 (July 2011): 943–50, doi:10.5665/SLEEP.1132.

24. Tracey Leigh Signal et al., "Scheduled Napping as a Countermeasure to Sleepiness in Air Traffic Controllers," *Journal of Sleep Research* 18, no. 1 (Feb 2009), doi:10.1111/j.1365-2869.2008.00702.x.

25. Shawn Achor and Michelle Gielan, "The Data-Driven Case for Vacation," *Harvard Business Review*, July 13, 2016, https://hbr.org/2016/07/the-data-driven-case-for-vacation.

26. "Comparing Meditation Techniques," Transcendental Meditation, last modified 2020, https://www.tm.org/meditation-techniques.

27. Antoine Lutz et al., "Regulation of the Neural Circuitry of Emotion by Compassion Meditation: Effects of Meditative Expertise," *PLOS One* 3, no. 3 (March 2008), doi:10.1371/journal.pone.0001897.

28. Mayo Clinic Staff, "Meditation: A Simple, Fast Way to Reduce Stress," Mayo Clinic, September 18, 2019, https://www.mayoclinic.org/tests-procedures/meditation/in-depth/meditation/art-20045858.

29. Lorenza S. Colzato, Ayca Ozturk, and Bernhard Hommel, "Meditate to Create: The Impact of Focused-Attention and Open-Monitoring Training on Convergent and Divergent Thinking," *Frontiers in Psychology* 3, no. 116 (Apr 2012), doi:10.3389/fpsyg.2012.00116.

30. Wake Forest Baptist Medical Center, "Demystifying Meditation: Brain Imaging Illustrates How Meditation Reduces Pain," ScienceDaily, April 11, 2011, https://www.sciencedaily.com/releases/2011/04/110405174835.htm.

31. Colin Allen, "The Benefits of Meditation," *Psychology Today*, updated June 9, 2016, https://www.psychologytoday.com/us/articles/200304/the-benefits-meditation.

32. Robert A. Emmons and Michael E. McCullough, "Counting Blessings Versus Burdens: An Experimental Investigation of Gratitude and Subjective Well-Being in Daily Life," *Journal of Personality and Social Psychology* 84, no. 2 (2003): 377–89, doi:10.1037/0022-3514.84.2.377.

33. "Giving Thanks Can Make You Happier," *HEALTHbeat* (newsletter), *Harvard Health Publishing*, accessed January 23, 2020, https://www.health.harvard.edu/healthbeat/giving-thanks-can-make-you-happier.

34. "An Experiment in Gratitude | The Science of Happiness," SoulPancake (YouTube video), July 11, 2013, https://www.youtube.com/watch?v=oHv6vTKD6lg.

35. Liz Mineo, "Good Genes Are Nice, But Joy Is Better," *The Harvard Gazette*, April 11, 2017, https://news.harvard.edu/gazette/story/2017/04/over-nearly-80-years-harvard-study-has-been-showing-how-to-live-a-healthy-and-happy-life/.

36. "5 Benefits of Healthy Relationships," *HealthBeat* (blog), Northwestern Medicine, https://www.nm.org/healthbeat/healthy-tips/5-benefits-of-healthy-relationships.

Chapter 2

1. Steven Novella, "Firewalk Mishap," *Neurologica* (blog), July 23, 2012, https://theness.com/neurologicablog/index.php/firewalk-mishap/.

2. Cristofer Jeschke, "Self-Help Books Don't Work — Here's Why," Medium, August 8, 2018, https://medium.com/@crisjeschke/self-help-books-dont-work-here-s-why-7737df3aa6e9.

3. Mark Manson, "5 Problems with the Self-Help Industry," *Mark Manson* (blog), accessed January 24, 2020, https://markmanson.net/self-help.

4. Kendra Cherry, "How People's Prejudices Develop," Verywell Mind, updated November 7, 2019, https://www.verywellmind.com/what-is-prejudice-2795476.

5. Anna Quindlen, "Flight Attendants: An Old Stereotype Is Given the Air," *New York Times*, April 24, 1978, https://www.nytimes.com/1978/04/24/archives/flight-attendants-an-old-stereotype-is-given-the-air-time-to-read-a.html.

6. William Arthur Ward Quotes, BrainyQuote.com, accessed January 24, 2020, https://www.brainyquote.com/quotes/william_arthur_ward_110017.

7. Carol Pogash, "A Self-Improvement Quest That Led to Burned Feet," *New York Times*, July 22, 2012, https://www.nytimes.com/2012/07/23/us/nearly-two-dozen-injured-at-tony-robbins-seminar.html.

8. Oliver Burkeman, "The Power of Negative Thinking," *New York Times*, August 4, 2012, https://www.nytimes.com/2012/08/05/opinion/sunday/the-positive-power-of-negative-thinking.html.

9. Bergink, "Happiness: It's Not Just Your Genes, Stupid!"

10. Jennifer Ouellette, "Come Firewalk With Me: The Physics of Hot Coals," *Cocktail Party Physics* (blog), *Scientific American*, July 24, 2012, https://blogs.scientificamerican.com/cocktail-party-physics/come-firewalk-with-me-the-physics-of-hot-coals/.

11. Gabriele Oettingen and Doris Mayer, "The Motivating Function of Thinking About the Future: Expectations Versus Fantasies," *Journal of Personality and Social Psychology* 83, no. 5 (2002): 1198–212, doi:10.1037//0022-3514.83.5.1198.

12. Jeremy Dean, "Success! Why Expectations Beat Fantasies," *PsyBlog* (blog), January 20, 2011, https://www.spring.org.uk/2011/01/success-why-expectations-beat-fantasies.php.

13. Joanne V. Wood, "Should We Re-think Positive Thinking?" *Psychology Today*, March 20, 2009, https://www.psychologytoday.com/us/blog/regarding-self-regard/200903/should-we-re-think-positive-thinking.

14. Tomas Chamorro-Premuzic, "Less-Confident People Are More Successful," *Harvard Business Review*, July 6, 2012, https://hbr.org/2012/07/less-confident-people-are-more-su.

15. "What Is Self-Compassion?" Center for Mindful Self-Compassion, accessed January 23, 2020, https://centerformsc.org/learn-msc/.

16. "The Power of Self-Compassion," *HEALTHbeat* (newsletter), *Harvard Health Publishing*, accessed January 23, 2020, https://www.health.harvard.edu/healthbeat/the-power-of-self-compassion.

17. C. S. von Bartheld, J. Bahney, and S. Herculano-Houzel, "The Search for True Numbers of Neurons and Glial Cells in the Human Brain: A Review of 150 Years of Cell Counting," *Journal of Comparative Neurology* 524, no. 18 (Dec 2016): 3865–895, doi:10.1002/cne.24040.

18. Eric R. Kandel et al., eds., *Principles of Neural Science,* 5th ed. (New York: McGraw-Hill, 2013).

19. Omri Weisman and Ruth Feldman, "Oxytocin Effects on the Human Brain: Findings, Questions, and Future Directions," *Biological Psychiatry* 74, no. 3 (Aug 2013): 158–59, doi:10.1016/j.biopsych.2013.05.026.

20. C. Sue Carter, "Oxytocin Pathways and the Evolution of Human Behavior," *Annual Review of Psychology* 65 (Jan 2014): 17–39, doi:10.1146/annurev-psych-010213-115110.

21. "Oxytocin," You and Your Hormones, last modified March 2015, https://www.yourhormones.info/hormones/oxytocin/.

22. Ed Yong, "The Weak Science Behind the Wrongly Named Moral Molecule," *Atlantic*, November 13, 2015, https://www.theatlantic.com/science/archive/2015/11/the-weak-science-of-the-wrongly-named-moral-molecule/415581/.

23. Ibid.

24. Carter, "Oxytocin Pathways and the Evolution of Human Behavior."

25. Roy A. Wise, "Dopamine, Learning and Motivation," *Nature Reviews Neuroscience* 5 (June 2004): 483–94, doi:10.1038/nrn1406.

26. Roy A. Wise and Pierre-Paul Rompré, "Brain Dopamine and Reward," *Annual Review of Psychology* 40 (Feb 1989): 191–225, doi:10.1146/annurev.ps.40.020189.001203.

Chapter 3

1. Lydia Dishman, "The Science of Why We Talk Too Much (and How to Shut Up)," *Fast Company*, June 11, 2015, https://www.fastcompany.com/3047285/the-science-of-why-we-talk-too-much-and-how-to-shut-up.

2. The Radicati Group, Inc., *Email Statistics Report, 2019–2023*, February 2019, https://www.radicati.com/wp/wp-content/uploads/2018/12/Email-Statistics-Report-2019-2023-Executive-Summary.pdf.

3. Andrew K. Przybylski and Netta Weinstein, "Can You Connect with Me Now? How the Presence of Mobile Communication Technology Influences Face-to-Face Conversation Quality," *Journal of Social and Personal Relationships* 30, no. 3 (July 2012): 237–46, doi:10.1177/0265407512453827.

4. Leon Watson, "Humans Have Shorter Attention Span Than Goldfish, Thanks to Smartphones," *Telegraph*, May 15, 2015, https://www.telegraph.co.uk/science/2016/03/12/humans-have-shorter-attention-span-than-goldfish-thanks-to-smart.

5. Carmine Gallo, "Why PowerPoint Presentations Always Die After 10 Minutes and How to Rescue Them," *Forbes*, April 30, 2013, https://www.forbes.com/sites/carminegallo/2014/04/30/why-powerpoint-presentations-always-die-after-10-minutes-and-how-to-rescue-them.

6. Joshua Freedman, "Back in Focus – Daniel Goleman and Joshua Freedman on Attention and Emotion, Part 2," Six Seconds, October 8, 2013, https://www.6seconds.org/2013/10/08/goleman-back-in-focus.

7. Rebecca Lake, "Listening Statistics: 23 Facts You Need to Hear," Credit Donkey, September 17, 2015, https://www.creditdonkey.com/listening-statistics.html.

8. John Medina, "The Brain Cannot Multitask," *Brain Rules* (blog), March 16, 2008, https://brainrules.blogspot.com/2008/03/brain-cannot-multitask_16.html.

9. Dick Lee and Delmar Hatesohl, "Listening: Our Most Used Communications Skill," University of Missouri Extension, reviewed October 1993, https://extension2.missouri.edu/cm150.

10. Jack Zenger and Joseph Folkman, "What Great Listeners Actually Do," *Harvard Business Review*, July 14, 2016, https://hbr.org/2016/07/what-great-listeners-actually-do.

11. Kevin McSpadden, "You Now Have a Shorter Attention Span Than a Goldfish," *Time*, May 14, 2015, https://time.com/3858309/attention-spans-goldfish.

12. Jolie Kerr, "How to Talk to People, According to Terry Gross," *New York Times*, November 17, 2018, https://www.nytimes.com/2018/11/17/style/self-care/terry-gross-conversation-advice.html.

13. Dave Isay, "How I Learned to Listen," *TEDBlog* (blog), March 4, 2015, https://blog.ted.com/how-i-learned-to-listen.

14. Ralph G. Nichols and Leonard A. Stevens, "Listening to People," *Harvard Business Review*, September 1957, https://hbr.org/1957/09/listening-to-people.

15. Abdullah Almaatouq et al., "Are You Your Friends' Friend? Poor Perception of Friendship Ties Limits the Ability to Promote Behavioral Change," *PLOS One* 11, no. 3 (Mar 2016), doi:10.1371/journal.pone.0151588.

16. Diana I. Tamir and Jason P. Mitchell, "Disclosing Information about the Self Is Intrinsically Rewarding," *Proceedings of the National Academy of Sciences of the United States of America* 109, no. 21 (May 2012): 8038–43, doi:10.1073/pnas.1202129109.

17. Marianna Pogosyan, "How We Talk and Listen Affects Our Relationships," *Psychology Today*, July 27, 2018, https://www.psychologytoday.com/us/blog/between-cultures/201807/how-we-talk-and-listen-affects-our-relationships.

18. Donella Caspersz and Ania Stasinska, "Can We Teach Effective Listening? An Exploratory Study," *Journal of University Teaching & Learning Practice* 12, no. 4 (2015), http://ro.uow.edu.au/jutlp/vol12/iss4/2.

19. Adrian F. Ward, "The Neuroscience of Everybody's Favorite Topic," *Scientific American*, July 16, 2013, https://www.scientificamerican.com/article/the-neuroscience-of-everybody-favorite-topic-themselves.

20. Robert B. Cialdini, "Harnessing the Science of Persuasion," *Harvard Business Review*, October 2001, https://hbr.org/2001/10/harnessing-the-science-of-persuasion.

Chapter 4

1. Todd B. Kashdan, Paul Rose, and Frank D. Fincham, "Curiosity and Exploration: Facilitating Positive Subjective Experiences and Personal Growth Opportunities," *Journal of Personality Assessment* 82, no. 3 (2004): 291–305, doi:10.1207/s15327752jpa8203_05.

2. Matthias J. Gruber, Bernard D. Gelman, and Charan Ranganath, "States of Curiosity Modulate Hippocampus-Dependent Learning via the Dopaminergic Circuit," *Neuron* 84, no. 2 (2014): 486–96, doi:10.1016/j.neuron.2014.08.060.

3. George Loewenstein, "The Psychology of Curiosity: A Review and Reinterpretation," *Psychological Bulletin* 116, no. 1 (1994): 75–98, doi:10.1037/0033-2909.116.1.75.

4. Annie Murphy Paul, "How to Stimulate Curiosity," *Time*, April 15, 2013, https://ideas.time.com/2013/04/15/how-to-stimulate-curiosity.

5. Basil Shikin, "The Importance of Hiring Curious People," *Forbes*, October 19, 2017, https://www.forbes.com/sites/forbestechcouncil/2017/10/19/the-importance-of-hiring-curious-people/#77107b8332c7.

6. Adam Robinson, "Want to Boost Your Bottom Line? Encourage Your Employees to Work on Side Projects," *Inc.*, March 12, 2018, https://www.inc.com/adam-robinson/google-employees-dedicate-20-percent-of-their-time-to-side-projects-heres-how-it-works.html.

7. Francesca Gino, "The Business Case for Curiosity," *Harvard Business Review*, September–October 2018, https://hbr.org/2018/09/curiosity.

8. Edmund Burke, *On the Sublime and Beautiful* (New York: P.F. Collier & Son, 1909–14).

9. Elias Baumgarten, "Curiosity as a Moral Virtue," *International Journal of Applied Philosophy* 15, no 2 (2001): 169–84, doi:10.5840/ijap200115215.

10. Todd B. Kashdan and Paul J. Silvia, "Curiosity and Interest: The Benefits of Thriving on Novelty and Challenge," in *The Oxford Handbook of Positive Psychology*, 2nd ed. (Oxford, UK: Oxford University Press, 2009), 367–74.

11. Susan Engel, "The Case for Curiosity," *Educational Leadership* 70, no. 5 (2013): 36–40.

12. Sophie von Stumm, Benedikt Hell, and Tomas Chamorro-Premuzic, "The Hungry Mind: Intellectual Curiosity Is the Third Pillar of Academic Performance," *Perspectives on Psychological Science* 6, no. 6 (2011): 574–88, doi:10.1177/1745691611421204.

13. Jordan Litman, "Curiosity and the Pleasures of Learning: Wanting and Liking New Information," *Cognition and Emotion* 19, no. 6 (2005): 793–814, doi:10.1080/02699930541000101.

14. Gruber, Gelman, and Ranganath, "States of Curiosity Modulate Hippocampus-Dependent Learning via the Dopaminergic Circuit."

15. Peter Roesler, "8 of the Biggest Business Mistakes in History," *Inc.*, April 20, 2015, https://www.inc.com/peter-roesler/8-of-the-biggest-business-mistakes-in-history.html.

16. "Excite.com Competitive Analysis, Marketing Mix, and Traffic," Alexa, accessed February 1, 2020, https://www.alexa.com/siteinfo/excite.com.

17. Roesler, "8 of the Biggest Business Mistakes in History."

18. Minda Zetlin, "Blockbuster Could Have Bought Netflix for $50 Million, but the CEO Thought It Was a Joke," *Inc.*, September 20, 2019, https://www.inc.com/minda-zetlin/netflix-blockbuster-meeting-marc-randolph-reed-hastings-john-antioco.html.

19. Tiffany Hsu, "The World's Last Blockbuster Has No Plans to Close," *New York Times*, March 6, 2019, https://www.nytimes.com/2019/03/06/business/last-blockbuster-store.html.

20. Gwen Wendenheimer, "10 Big Companies Killed By One Mistake," Business Pundit, August 21, 2018, http://www.businesspundit.com/big-companies-one-mistake.

21. Pamela N. Danziger, "The Fall of the Mall and How to Make Them Rise Again," *Forbes*, October 14, 2018, https://www.forbes.com/sites/pamdanziger/2018/10/14/the-fall-of-the-mall-and-three-ways-to-make-them-rise-again/#2fd203c72a26.

22. Mengqi, Sun, "What Pushed Radio Shack into Bankruptcy?" *Christian Science Monitor*, March 10, 2017, https://www.csmonitor.com/Business/2017/0310/What-pushed-Radio-Shack-into-bankruptcy.

23. Gary E. Swan and Dorit Carmelli, "Curiosity and Mortality in Aging Adults: A 5-Year Follow-up of the Western Collaborative Group Study," *Psychology and Aging* 11, no. 3: 449–53, doi:10.1037/0882-7974.11.3.449.

24. Todd B. Kashdan and Michael F. Steger, "Curiosity and Pathways to Well-being and Meaning in Life: Traits, States, and Everyday Behaviors," *Motivation and Emotion* 31, no. 3 (2007): 159–73.

25. James R. Rodrigue, Kenneth R. Olson, and Robert P. Markley, "Induced Mood and Curiosity," *Cognitive Therapy and Research* 11, no. 1 (1987): 101–106, doi:10.1007/BF01183135.

26. Evan Polman, Rachel L. Ruttan, and Joann Peck, "Using Curiosity to Increase the Choice of 'Should' Options," American Psychological Association, press release, August 2016, https://www.apa.org/news/press/releases/2016/08/using-curiosity.pdf.

27. Todd B. Kashdan, "The Power of Curiosity," *Experience Life*, May 2010, https://experiencelife.com/article/the-power-of-curiosity.

28. Jennifer S. Holland, "Why Asking Questions and Embracing Uncertainty Is Good for You," June 3, 2010, AARP, https://www.aarp.org/entertainment/books/info-06-2010/the_author_speaks_how_asking_questions_and_being_nosy_awakens_the_spirit_.html.

29. Baumgarten, "Curiosity as a Moral Virtue."

30. Todd B. Kashdan and John E. Roberts, "Trait and State Curiosity in the Genesis of Intimacy: Differentiation From Related Constructs," *Journal of Social and Clinical Psychology* 23, no. 6 (2004): 792–816, doi:10.1521/jscp.23.6.792.54800.

31. Jill Suttie, "Why Curious People Have Better Relationships," *Greater Good Magazine*, May 31, 2017,

https://greatergood.berkeley.edu/article/item/why_curious_people_have_better_rel
ationships.

32. Todd B. Kashdan et al., "When Curiosity Breeds Intimacy: Taking Advantage of
Intimacy Opportunities and Transforming Boring Conversations," *Journal of
Personality* 79, no. 6 (2011): 1369–402, doi:10.1111/j.1467-6494.2010.00697.x.

33. Todd B. Kashdan and John E. Roberts, "Affective Outcomes in Superficial and
Intimate Interactions: Roles of Social Anxiety and Curiosity," *Journal of Research in
Personality* 40, no. 2 (April 2006): 140–67, doi:10.1016/j.jrp.2004.10.005.

34. Freda-Marie Hartung and Britta Renner, "Social Curiosity and Interpersonal
Perception: A Judge × Trait Interaction," *Personality and Social Psychology Bulletin*
37, no 6 (2011): 796–814, doi:10.1177/0146167211400618.

35. Roman Krznaric, "Six Habits of Highly Empathic People," *Greater Good Magazine*,
September 7, 2012,
https://greatergood.berkeley.edu/article/item/six_habits_of_highly_empathic_peop
le1.

36. Diana I. Cordova and Mark R. Lepper, "Intrinsic Motivation and the Process of
Learning: Beneficial Effects of Contextualization, Personalization, and Choice,"
Journal of Educational Psychology 88, no. 4 (1996): 715–30: doi:10.1037/0022-
0663.88.4.715.

37. Aaron E. Black and Edward L. Deci, "The Effects of Instructors' Autonomy Support
and Students' Autonomous Motivation on Learning Organic Chemistry: A Self-
Determination Theory Perspective," *Science Education* 84, no. 6 (2000): 740–56,
doi:10.1002/1098-237X(200011)84:6<740::AID-SCE4>3.0.CO;2-3.

38. Andrew J. Elliot et al., "Competence Valuation as a Strategic Intrinsic Motivation
Process," *Personality and Social Psychology Bulletin* 26, no. 7 (July 2000): 780–94,
doi:10.1177/0146167200269004.

39. Kashdan, Rose, and Fincham, "Curiosity and Exploration: Facilitating Positive
Subjective Experiences and Personal Growth Opportunities."

Chapter 5

1. Rebecca Knight, "How to Be Good at Managing Both Introverts and Extroverts,"
Harvard Business Review, November 16, 2015, https://hbr.org/2015/11/how-to-be-
good-at-managing-both-introverts-and-extroverts.

2. "Jungian Type Inventory," ChangingMinds.org, accessed February 2, 2020,
http://changingminds.org/explanations/preferences/mbti.htm.

3. "Extraversion or Introversion," The Myers & Briggs Foundation, accessed February 2,
2020, https://www.myersbriggs.org/my-mbti-personality-type/mbti-
basics/extraversion-or-introversion.htm?bhcp=1.

4. "Extraversion and Introversion," Psychologist World, accessed February 2, 2020,
https://www.psychologistworld.com/influence-personality/extraversion-introversion.

5. Anna Domanska, "Introvert Leaders vs Extrovert Leaders: Review of Leadership
Styles," *Industry Leaders*, May 30, 2016,
https://www.industryleadersmagazine.com/introvert-leaders-vs-extrovert-leaders-
review-leadership-styles.

6. Sophia Dembling, "Are Introverts Better Friends Than Extroverts?" *Psychology
Today*, January 22, 2018, https://www.psychologytoday.com/us/blog/the-introverts-
corner/201801/are-introverts-better-friends-extroverts.

7. Michael Koh, "6 Things Every Introvert Has to Secretly Deal With," Thought Catalog, April 5, 2014, https://thoughtcatalog.com/michael-koh/2014/04/6-things-every-introvert-has-to-secretly-deal-with.

8. H. J. Eysenck, "The Inheritance of Extraversion-Introversion," *Acta Psychologica* 12 (1956): 95–110, doi:10.1016/0001-6918(56)90010-5.

9. H. J. Eysenck, "Crime and Personality," *Medico-Legal Journal* 47, no. 1 (1979): 18–32, doi:10.1177/002581727904700104.

10. Roberta Riccelli et al., "Surface-Based Morphometry Reveals the Neuroanatomical Basis of the Five-Factor Model of Personality," *Social Cognitive and Affective Neuroscience* 12, no. 4 (April 2017): 671–84, doi:10.1093/scan/nsw175.

11. Xu Lei, Tianliang Yang, and Taoyu Wu, "Functional Neuroimaging of Extraversion-Introversion," *Neuroscience Bulletin* 31, no. 6 (Dec 2015): 663–75, doi:10.1007/s12264-015-1565-1.

12. R. A. Depue and P. F. Collins, "Neurobiology of the Structure of Personality: Dopamine, Facilitation of Incentive Motivation, and Extraversion," *Behavioral and Brain Sciences* 22, no. 3 (June 1999): 491–517, doi:10.1017/s0140525x99002046.

13. Michael X. Cohen et al., "Individual Differences in Extraversion and Dopamine Genetics Predict Neural Reward Responses," *Cognitive Brain Research* 25, no. 3 (Dec 2005): 851–61, doi:10.1016/j.cogbrainres.2005.09.018.

14. Depue and Collins, "Neurobiology of the Structure of Personality: Dopamine, Facilitation of Incentive Motivation, and Extraversion."

15. Kendra Cherry, "Discovery and Functions of Acetylcholine," Verywell Mind, October 9, 2019, https://www.verywellmind.com/what-is-acetylcholine-2794810.

16. Jennifer Granneman, "Why Introverts and Extroverts Are Different: The Science," Quiet Revolution, accessed February 2, 2020, https://www.quietrev.com/why-introverts-and-extroverts-are-different-the-science.

17. "Extraversion or Introversion," The Myers & Briggs Foundation.

18. Elaine Houston, "Introvert vs Extrovert: A Look at the Spectrum and Psychology," PositivePsychology.com, April 7, 2019, https://positivepsychology.com/introversion-extroversion-spectrum.

19. Adam M. Grant, "Rethinking the Extraverted Sales Ideal: The Ambivert Advantage," *Psychological Science* 24, no. 6 (2013): 1024–30, doi:10.1177/0956797612463706.

20. Knight, "How to Be Good at Managing Both Introverts and Extroverts."

21. Depue and Collins, "Neurobiology of the Structure of Personality: Dopamine, Facilitation of Incentive Motivation, and Extraversion."

22. V. De Pascalis, "On the Psychophysiology of Extraversion," in *On the Psychobiology of Personality* (Amsterdam: Elsevier, 2004),

23. Adam M. Grant, "5 Myths About Introverts and Extroverts," Quiet Revolution, accessed February 2, 2020, https://www.quietrev.com/5-myths-about-introverts-and-extroverts.

24. Adam M. Grant, "Say Goodbye to MBTI, the Fad That Won't Die," LinkedIn, September 17, 2013, https://www.linkedin.com/pulse/20130917155206-69244073-say-goodbye-to-mbti-the-fad-that-won-t-die.

25. Roy F. Baumeister and Mark R. Leary, "The Need to Belong: Desire for Interpersonal Attachments as a Fundamental Human Motivation," *Psychological Bulletin* 117, no. 3 (1995): 497–529, doi:10.1037/0033-2909.117.3.497.

26. William Pavot, Ed Diener, and Frank Fujita, "Extraversion and Happiness," *Personality and Individual Differences* 11, no. 12 (1990): 1299–306, doi:10.1016/0191-8869(90)90157-M.

27. Peter D. MacIntyre and Kimly A. Thivierge, "The Effects of Speaker Personality on Anticipated Reactions to Public Speaking," *Communication Research Reports* 12, no. 2 (1995): 125–33, doi:10.1080/08824099509362048.

28. Susan Cain, "An Introvert Steps Out," *New York Times*, April 27, 2012, https://www.nytimes.com/2012/04/29/books/review/how-the-author-of-quiet-delivered-a-rousing-speech.html.

29. Susan Cain, "Public Speaking for Introverts: Tip #1 (Courtesy of Malcolm Gladwell)" Quiet Revolution, accessed February 2, 2020, https://www.quietrev.com/public-speaking-for-introverts-tip-1-courtesy-of-malcolm-gladwell.

30. Adam Grant, Francesca Gino, and David A. Hofmann, "The Hidden Advantages of Quiet Bosses," *Harvard Business Review*, December 2010, https://hbr.org/2010/12/the-hidden-advantages-of-quiet-bosses.

31. Francesca Gino, "Introverts, Extroverts, and the Complexities of Team Dynamics," *Harvard Business Review*, March 16, 2015, https://hbr.org/2015/03/introverts-extroverts-and-the-complexities-of-team-dynamics.

32. "Video: How Brainwriting Can Neutralize the Loudmouths," Northwestern Kellogg, June 26, 2014, https://www.kellogg.northwestern.edu/news_articles/2014/06262014-video-thompson-brainwriting.aspx.

33. Knight, "How to Be Good at Managing Both Introverts and Extroverts."

34. "Coping as an Introvert in an Extrovert World," Mechanics of "Why?" accessed February 2, 2020, http://mechanicsofwhy.com/problems/others/coping-as-an-introvert-in-an-extrovert-world.

35. Judith E. Glaser, "Conversational Blind Spots," *Psychology Today*, October 30, 2014, https://www.psychologytoday.com/us/blog/conversational-intelligence/201410/conversational-blind-spots-0.

36. Jennifer Granneman, "All the Possible Reasons I'm Not Talking Right Now," Introvert, Dear, July 27, 2018, https://introvertdear.com/news/all-the-possible-reasons-im-not-talking-right-now.

37. Brian R. Little, "Personal Projects and Free Traits: Personality and Motivation Reconsidered," *Social and Personality Psychology Compass* 2, no. 3 (2008): 1235–254, doi:10.1111/j.1751-9004.2008.00106.x.

38. William Fleeson, Adriane B. Malanos, and Noelle M. Achille, "An Intraindividual Process Approach to the Relationship between Extraversion and Positive Affect: Is Acting Extraverted as 'Good' as Being Extraverted?" *Journal of Personality and Social Psychology* 83, no. 6 (2002): 1409–22, doi:10.1037/0022-3514.83.6.1409.

39. "C. G. Jung Quotes," Goodreads, accessed February 2, 2020, https://www.goodreads.com/quotes/23089-the-meeting-of-two-personalities-is-like-the-contact-of.

Chapter 6

1. Lionel Trilling, *Sincerity and Authenticity* (Cambridge, MA: Harvard University Press, 1972).

2. Karyn Fish, Kathrin Rothermich, and Marc D. Pell, "The Sound of (In)Sincerity," *Journal of Pragmatics* 121 (2017), doi:10.1016/j.pragma.2017.10.008.

3. Roy F. Baumeister, "How the Self Became a Problem: A Psychological Review of Historical Research," *Journal of Personality and Social Psychology* 52, no. 1 (1987): 163–176, doi:10.1037/0022-3514.52.1.163.

4. David Sudar, "Authenticity vs Sincerity," *Path of Sincerity* (blog), May 14, 2016, https://www.pathofsincerity.com/authenticity-vs-sincerity.

5. Adam Kelly, "Dialectic of Sincerity: Lionel Trilling and David Foster Wallace," October 17, 2014, Post45, http://post45.org/2014/10/dialectic-of-sincerity-lionel-trilling-and-david-foster-wallace.

6. Thomas Frank, *The Conquest of Cool: Business Culture, Counterculture, and the Rise of Hip Consumerism* (Chicago: University of Chicago Press, 1998).

7. Sandra Gountas, Michael T. Ewing, and John I. Gountas, "Exploring Consumers' Responses to Service Providers' Positive Affective Displays," *International Journal of Culture Tourism and Hospitality Research* 1, no. 1 (April 2007): 97–109, doi:10.1108/17506180710729637.

8. Jason Perepelkin and David Di Zhang, "Quality Alone Is Not Enough to Be Trustworthy: The Mediating Role of Sincerity Perception," *International Journal of Pharmaceutical and Healthcare Marketing* 8, no. 2 (June 2014):226–42, doi:10.1108/IJPHM-02-2013-0006.

9. Edward C. Bursk, "Low-Pressure Selling," *Harvard Business Review*, July–August 2006, https://hbr.org/2006/07/low-pressure-selling.

10. Abdullah Demirel and Irem Eren Erdogmus, "The Impacts of Fans' Sincerity Perceptions and Social Media Usage on Attitude toward Sponsor," *Sport, Business and Management: An International Journal* 6, no. 1 (March 2016): 36–54, doi:10.1108/SBM-07-2014-0036.

11. Stephen J. Dubner, "Sincerity Is the Key to Effective Leadership," *The Art of Productions*, September 10, 2014, https://www.theartof.com/videos/sincerity-is-the-key-to-effective-leadership.

12. Michael Wenzel et al., "The Mandate of the Collective: Apology Representativeness Determines Perceived Sincerity and Forgiveness in Intergroup Contexts," *Personality and Social Psychology Bulletin* 43, no. 6 (2017): 758–771, doi:10.1177/0146167217697093.

13. Adriana F. Kraig et al., "The Neurophysiology of Corporate Apologies: Why Do People Believe Insincere Apologies?" *International Journal of Business Communication* (July 2019), doi:10.1177/2329488419858391.

14. Tessa E. Basford, "Leader Apologies: How Content and Delivery Influence Sincerity Appraisals," *International Journal of Business and Social Science* 4, no. 5 (May 2013): 9–26.

15. Joyce L. T. Leong, "Is Gratitude Always Beneficial to Interpersonal Relationships? The Interplay of Grateful Disposition, Grateful Mood, and Grateful Expression Among Married Couples," *Personality and Social Psychology Bulletin* 46, no 1 (Jan 2020): 64–78, doi:10.1177/0146167219842868.

16. Guy Foster Bachman and Laura K. Guerrero, "Forgiveness, Apology, and Communicative Responses to Hurtful Events," *Communication Reports* 19, no. 1 (2006): 45–56, doi:10.1080/08934210600586357.

17. Andy J. Merolla, "Forgive Like You Mean It: Sincerity of Forgiveness and the Experience of Negative Affect," *Communication Quarterly* 62, no. 1 (2014): 36–56, doi:10.1080/01463373.2013.860903.

18. Karina Schumann, "Does Love Mean Never Having to Say You're Sorry? Associations between Relationship Satisfaction, Perceived Apology Sincerity, and Forgiveness,"

Journal of Social and Personal Relationships 29, no. 7 (2012): 997–1010, doi:10.1177/0265407512448277.

19. Christine Moorman, Rohit Deshpande, and Gerald Zaltman, "Factors Affecting Trust in Market Research Relationships," *Journal of Marketing* 57, no. 1 (1993): 81–101, doi:10.1177/002224299305700106.

20. Alixandra Barasch, Jonathan Z. Berman, and Deborah A. Small, "When Payment Undermines the Pitch: On the Persuasiveness of Pure Motives in Fund-Raising," *Psychological Science* 27, no. 10 (2016): 1388–97, doi:10.1177/0956797616638841.

21. Niek Hoogervorst et al., "How Perceptions of Altruism and Sincerity Affect Client Trust in Volunteers Versus Paid Workers," *Nonprofit and Voluntary Sector Quarterly* 45, no. 3 (2016): 593–611, doi:10.1177/0899764015597778.

22. Robert J. Bies, "Beyond 'Voice': The Influence of Decision-Maker Justification and Sincerity on Procedural Fairness Judgments," *Representative Research in Social Psychology* 17, no. 1 (1987): 3–14.

23. Kevin P. Durkin and Colin H. Dunn, "Building Your Case for the Jury," *Journal of the Section of Litigation* 36, no. 3 (Spring 2010): 43–52.

Chapter 7

1. Marc D. Hauser, *Evolution of Communication* (Cambridge, MA: MIT Press, 1996),

2. Robert C. Berwick and Noam Chomsky, *Why Only Us: Language and Evolution* (Cambridge, MA: MIT Press, 2017)

3. E. T. Klemmer and F. W. Snyder, "Measurement of Time Spent Communicating," *Journal of Communication* 22, no. 2 (1972): 142–158, doi:10.1111/j.1460-2466.1972.tb00141.x.

4. Mor Naaman, Jeffrey Boase, and Chih-Hui Lai, "Is It Really About Me? Message Content in Social Awareness Streams," *CSCW '10* (Feb 2010): 189–92, doi:10.1145/1718918.1718953.

5. Jeffrey H. Dyer, Hal Gregersen, and Clayton M. Christensen, "The Innovator's DNA" *Harvard Business Review*, December 2009, https://hbr.org/2009/12/the-innovators-dna.

6. Larry Ferlazzo, "'A More Beautiful Question': An Interview With Warren Berger," *Classroom Q&A with Larry Ferlazzo* (blog), July 16, 2014, https://blogs.edweek.org/teachers/classroom_qa_with_larry_ferlazzo/2014/07/a_more_beautiful_question_an_interview_with_warren_berger.html.

7. Nancy L. Collins and Lynn Carol Miller, "Self-Disclosure and Liking: A Meta-Analytic Review 116, no. 3 (1994): 457–75, doi:10.1037/0033-2909.116.3.457.

8. Azy Barak and Orit Gluck-Ofri, "Degree and Reciprocity of Self-Disclosure in Online Forums, *CyberPsychology & Behavior* 10, no. 3 (2007): 407–17, doi:10.1089/cpb.2006.9938.

9. Diana I. Tamir and Jason P. Mitchell, "Disclosing Information about the Self Is Intrinsically Rewarding," *Proceedings of the National Academy of Sciences* 109, no. 21 (May 2012): 8038–43, doi:10.1073/pnas.1202129109.

10. Kandel et al. (ed.), *Principles of Neural Science,*

11. Wise and Rompré, "Brain Dopamine and Reward."

12. Yalda T. Uhls, *Media Moms & Digital Dads: A Fact-Not-Fear Approach to Parenting in the Digital Age* (Abingdon, UK: Routledge, 2016),

13. Brett McKay and Kate McKay, "How to Avoid Conversational Narcissism," The Art of Manliness, January 24, 2020, https://www.artofmanliness.com/articles/the-art-of-conversation-how-to-avoid-conversational-narcissism.

14. Charles Derber, *The Pursuit of Attention: Power and Ego in Everyday Life*, 2nd ed. (Oxford, UK: Oxford University Press, 2000).

15. Judith E. Glaser, "Blind Spots," *Psychology Today*, May 4, 2017, https://www.psychologytoday.com/us/blog/conversational-intelligence/201705/blind-spots.

16. Katrina Koslov et al., "Greater Left Resting Intracortical Activity as a Buffer to Social Threat," *Psychological Science* 22, no. 5 (2011): 641–49, doi:10.1177/0956797611403156.

17. Patricia Fripp, "The 5 Secrets of an Effective Sales Story," *Patricia Fripp* (blog), accessed February 3, 2020, https://www.fripp.com/5-secrets-effective-sales-story.

18. Barry Moltz, "The Power of Storytelling for Your Business," *Business Trends and Insights* (blog), *American Express*, July 16, 2014, https://www.americanexpress.com/en-us/business/trends-and-insights/articles/the-power-of-storytelling-for-your-business.

19. Kathi Kruse, "The Power of Storytelling to Connect, Build Trust and Close Sales," *Kruse Control Inc* (blog), November 17, 2014, https://www.krusecontrolinc.com/power-of-storytelling-to-connect-trust-close-sales.

20. Paul J. Zak, "How Stories Change the Brain," *Greater Good Magazine*, December 17, 2013, https://greatergood.berkeley.edu/article/item/how_stories_change_brain.

21. Kashdan and Fincham, "Facilitating Curiosity: A Social and Self-Regulatory Perspective for Scientifically Based Interventions."

22. Michael Heilman and Noah A. Smith, "Good Question! Statistical Ranking for Question Generation," *Human Language Technologies: The 2010 Annual Conference of the North American Chapter of the Association for Computational Linguistics* (June 2010): 609–17.

23. Linda Graham, "Stoplight Exercise Gives a Green Light to Learning," *Linda Graham, MFT* (blog), accessed February 3, 2020, https://lindagraham-mft.net/stoplight-exercise-gives-a-green-light-to-learning.

Chapter 8

1. Tamir and Mitchell, "Disclosing Information about the Self Is Intrinsically Rewarding."

2. Bo Feng and Eran Magen, "Relationship Closeness Predicts Unsolicited Advice Giving in Supportive Interactions," *Journal of Social and Personal Relationships* 33, no. 6 (2016), 751–67, doi:10.1177/0265407515592262.

3. Justin Kruger and David Dunning, "Unskilled and Unaware of It: How Difficulties in Recognizing One's Own Incompetence Lead to Inflated Self-Assessments," *Journal of Personality and Social Psychology* 77, no. 6 (Dec 1999): 1121–34, doi:10.1037//0022-3514.77.6.1121.

4. Heidi van Rooyen, Kevin Durrheim, and Graham Lindegger, "Advice-Giving Difficulties in Voluntary Counselling and Testing: A Distinctly Moral Activity," *AIDS Care: Psychological and Socio-medical Aspects of AIDS/HIV* 23, no. 3 (2011): 281–86, doi:10.1080/09540121.2010.507755.

5. Shai Danziger, Ronit Montal, and Rachel Barkan, "Idealistic Advice and Pragmatic Choice: A Psychological Distance Account," *Journal of Personality and Social Psychology* 102, no. 6 (2012): 1105–17, doi:10.1037/a0027013.

6. Ilan Yaniv and Shoham Choshen-Hillel, "When Guessing What Another Person Would Say Is Better Than Giving Your Own Opinion: Using Perspective-Taking to Improve Advice-Taking," *Journal of Experimental Social Psychology* 48, no. 5 (Sep 2012): 1022–28, doi:10.1016/j.jesp.2012.03.016.

7. Philip J. Mazzocco et al., "This Story Is Not for Everyone: Transportability and Narrative Persuasion," *Social Psychological and Personality Science* 1, no. 4 (2010): 361–68, doi:10.1177/1948550610376600.

8. Matthew D. Lieberman, "2017: What Scientific Term or Concept Ought to Be More Widely Known?" Edge.org, accessed February 3, 2020, https://www.edge.org/response-detail/27006.

9. Lee Ross and Andrew Ward, "Naïve Realism in Everyday Life: Implications for Social Conflict and Misunderstanding," in *Values and Knowledge*, ed. Edward S. Reed, Elliott Turiel, and Terrance Brown (London: Psychology Press, 2013), 103–36.

10. Thomas Gilovich and Lee Ross, *The Wisest One in the Room: How You Can Benefit from Social Psychology's Most Powerful Insights* (New York: Free Press, 2015).

11. Dan M. Kahan et al., "'They Saw a Protest': Cognitive Illiberalism and the Speech-Conduct Distinction," *Stanford Law Review* 64, no. 4 (Feb 2011): 851–906.

12. Orin Kerr, "People Believe What Resonates with Their Beliefs: An Interesting Experiment," *The Volokh Conspiracy* (blog), Reason.com, February 8, 2011, http://volokh.com/2011/02/08/people-believe-what-resonates-with-their-beliefs-an-interesting-experiment.

13. Robert J. Robinson et al., "Actual Versus Assumed Differences in Construal: 'Naive Realism' in Intergroup Perception and Conflict," *Journal of Personality and Social Psychology* 68, no. 3, 404–17, doi:10.1037/0022-3514.68.3.404.

14. Julie Biegner, "Stress Awareness: Boost Happiness, Not Cortisol," *The Wellness* (blog), accessed February 3, 2020, https://www.humnutrition.com/blog/stress-awareness-day-boost-happiness-lower-cortisol.

15. "Understanding the Stress Response," *Harvard Health Publishing*, updated May 1, 2018, https://www.health.harvard.edu/staying-healthy/understanding-the-stress-response.

16. Robert P. Abelson et al., eds., *Theories of Cognitive Consistency: A Sourcebook* (Chicago: Rand McNally, 1968),

17. Mark J. Perry, "More Evidence That It's Very Hard to 'Beat the Market' Over Time, 95% of Finance Professionals Can't Do It," *Carpe Diem* (blog), American Enterprise Institute, March 20, 2018, https://www.aei.org/carpe-diem/more-evidence-that-its-very-hard-to-beat-the-market-over-time-95-of-financial-professionals-cant-do-it.

18. Tamir and Mitchell, "Disclosing Information about the Self Is Intrinsically Rewarding."

19. Bo Feng, "When Should Advice Be Given? Assessing the Role of Sequential Placement of Advice in Supportive Interactions in Two Cultures," *Communication Research* 41, no. 7 (2014): 913–34, doi:10.1177/0093650212456203.

20. "The Anti-Vaccination Movement," Measles & Rubella Initiative, accessed February 3, 2020, https://measlesrubellainitiative.org/anti-vaccination-movement.

21. "Measles (Rubeola) Cases and Outbreaks," Centers for Disease Control and Prevention, updated February 3, 2020, https://www.cdc.gov/measles/cases-outbreaks.html.

22. "Vaccines and Preventable Diseases: What Everyone Should Know," Centers for Disease Control and Prevention, updated March 28, 2019, https://www.cdc.gov/vaccines/vpd/mmr/public/index.html.

23. Jeffrey S. Gerber and Paul A. Offit, "Vaccines and Autism: A Tale of Shifting Hypotheses," *Clinical Infectious Diseases* 48, no. 4 (Feb 2009): 456–61, doi:10.1086/596476.

24. Julie Leask et al., "Communicating with Parents about Vaccination: A Framework for Health Professionals," *BMC Pediatrics* 12, 154 (2012), doi:10.1186/1471-2431-12-154.

25. Dorothy R. Novick, "Why a Philly Pediatrician Seeks Common Ground with Vaccine-Hesitant Parents," *Philadelphia Inquirer*, updated May 15, 2019, https://www.inquirer.com/health/measles-vaccine-preventable-deaths-philadelphia-pediatrician-20190515.html.

26. Andrea L. Benin, "Qualitative Analysis of Mothers' Decision-Making About Vaccines for Infants: The Importance of Trust," *Pediatrics* 117, no. 5 (May 2006): 1532–41, doi:10.1542/peds.2005-1728.

27. Francesca Gino and Maurice E. Schweitzer, "Blinded by Anger or Feeling the Love: How Emotions Influence Advice Taking," *Journal of Applied Psychology* 93, no. 5 (2008): 1165–73, doi:10.1037/0021-9010.93.5.1165.

Chapter 9

1. Aimee Lutkin, "How to Really Listen in Conversation," Life Hacker, May 23, 2018, https://lifehacker.com/how-to-really-listen-in-conversations-1826204542.

2. Jonathan R. Cohen, "Open-Minded Listening," *Charlotte Law Review* (2014): 139–64, http://scholarship.law.ufl.edu/facultypub/464.

3. Anna Włoszczak-Szubzda and Miroslaw Jerzy Jarosz, "Professional Communication Competences of Nurses," *Annals of Agricultural and Environmental Medicine* 19, no. 3 (2012): 601–7.

4. Dana Heller Levitt, "Active Listening and Counselor Self-Efficacy," *The Clinical Supervisor* 20, no. 2 (2002): 101–15, doi:10.1300/J001v20n02_09.

5. Rosemary P. Ramsey and Ravipreet S. Sohi, "Listening to Your Customers: The Impact of Perceived Salesperson Listening Behavior on Relationship Outcomes," *Journal of the* Academy of Marketing Science 25, no. 127 (Mar 1997), doi:10.1007/BF02894348.

6. Harvey Wallace and Cliff Roberson, *Written and Interpersonal Communication: Methods for Law Enforcement*, 5th ed. (London: Pearson, 2012),

7. Blake J. Neff, *A Pastor's Guide to Interpersonal Communication* (Abingdon, UK: Routledge, 2006),

8. Graham D. Bodie, "The Understudied Nature of Listening in Interpersonal Communication: Introduction to a Special Issue," *International Journal of Listening* 25, no. 1–2 (2011): 1–9, doi:10.1080/10904018.2011.536462.

9. "Listening Effectively," Raj Soin College of Business Wright State University, accessed February 3, 2020, http://www.wright.edu/~scott.williams/skills/listening.htm.

10. Ram Charan, "The Discipline of Listening," *Harvard Business Review*, June 21, 2012, https://hbr.org/2012/06/the-discipline-of-listening.

11. Sara Lindberg, "What's the Difference between Hearing and Listening?" Healthline, September 26, 2018, https://www.healthline.com/health/hearing-vs-listening.

12. Jennifer Boyenga, "Listening vs. Hearing," Indian Hills Community College, accessed February 3, 2020, http://www.indianhills.edu/_myhills/courses/SPC101/documents/lu05_listening.pdf.

13. Harry Weger, Jr., Gina R. Castle, and Melissa C. Emmett, "Active Listening in Peer Interviews: The Influence of Message Paraphrasing on Perceptions of Listening Skill,"

International Journal of Listening 24, no. 1 (2010): 34–49, doi:10.1080/10904010903466311.

14. Kathryn Robertson, "Active Listening: More Than Just Paying Attention," *Australian Family Physician* 34, no. 12 (2005): 1053–55.

15. Yulia E. Chentsova-Dutton and Alexandra Vaughn, "Let Me Tell You What to Do: Cultural Differences in Advice-Giving," *Journal of Cross-Cultural Psychology* 43, no. 5 (2012): 687–703, doi:10.1177/0022022111402343.

16. George Simon, "Selective Listening and Attention: Hearing What You Want to Hear as a Manipulation Tactic," CounsellingResource.com, March 30, 2009, https://counsellingresource.com/features/2009/03/30/selective-listening.

17. T. Rinne et al., "Auditory Selective Attention Modulates Activation of Human Inferior Colliculus," *Journal of Neurophysiology* 100, no. 6 (Dec 2008): 3323–27, doi:10.1152/jn.90607.2008.

18. Prabhjot Singh and Niyum Gandhi, "Listening Is a Lost Art in Medicine. Here's How to Rediscover It," *Harvard Business Review*, November 6, 2017, https://hbr.org/2017/11/listening-is-a-lost-art-in-medicine-heres-how-to-rediscover-it.

19. Monisha Pasupathi et al., "Responsive Listening in Long-Married Couples: A Psycholinguistic Perspective," *Journal of Nonverbal Behavior* 23, no. 2 (June 1999): 173–93, doi:10.1023/A:1021439627043.

20. Loretta L. Pecchioni and Kelby K. Halone, "Relational Listening II: Form & Variation across Social and Personal Relationships," *International Journal of Listening* 14, no. 1 (2000): 69–93, doi:10.1080/10904018.2000.10499036.

21. S. Mineyama, "Supervisors' Attitudes and Skills for Active Listening with Regard to Working Conditions and Psychological Stress Reactions among Subordinate Workers," *Journal of Occupational Health* 49, no. 2 (Mar 2007): 81–87, doi:10.1539/joh.49.81.

22. Norio Mishima, Shinya Kubota, and Shoji Nagata, "The Development of a Questionnaire to Assess the Attitude of Active Listening," *Journal of Occupational Health* 42, no. 3 (May 2000): 111–18, doi:10.1539/joh.42.111.

23. Graham D. Bodie, "The Active-Empathic Listening Scale (AELS): Conceptualization and Evidence of Validity with the Interpersonal Domain," *Communication Quarterly* 59, no. 3 (2011): 277–95, doi:10.1080/01463373.2011.583495.

24. Thijs Fassaert et al., "Active Listening in Medical Consultations: Development of the Active Listening Observation Scale (ALOS-global)," *Patient Education and Counseling* 68, no. 3 (Dec 2007): 258–64, doi:10.1016/j.pec.2007.06.011.

25. Tonja Jacobi and Dylan Schweers, "Justice, Interrupted: The Effect of Gender, Ideology and Seniority at Supreme Court Oral Arguments," Virginia Law Review 103 (2017): 1379–496.

26. Teal Burrell, "The Science Behind Interrupting: Gender, Nationality and Power, and the Roles They Play," *Post Magazine*, March 14, 2018, https://www.scmp.com/magazines/post-magazine/long-reads/article/2137023/science-behind-interrupting-gender-nationality.

27. Lennox Morrison, "The Subtle Power of Uncomfortable Silences," *BBC Worklife*, July 18, 2017, https://www.bbc.com/worklife/article/20170718-the-subtle-power-of-uncomfortable-silences.

28. Sarah Trenholm and Arthur Jensen, *Interpersonal Communication*, 7th ed. (Oxford, UK: Oxford University Press, 2011),

29. J. B. Bavelas, L. Coates, and T. Johnson, "Listeners as Co-narrators," *Journal of Personality and Social Psychology* 79, no. 6 (Dec 2000): 941–52, doi:10.1037//0022-3514.79.6.941.

30. Joseph A. DeVito, *The Interpersonal Communication Book,* 15th ed. (London: Pearson, 2019),

31. Carl R. Rogers and Richard Evans Farson, *Active Listening* (Eastford, CT: Martino, 2015),

32. David McNaughton et al., "Learning to Listen: Teaching an Active Listening Strategy to Preservice Education Professionals," *Topics in Early Childhood Special Education* 27, no. 4 (2008): 223–31, doi:10.1177/0271121407311241.

Chapter 10

1. J. L. Taylor, "Proprioception," in *Encyclopedia of Neuroscience* (Amsterdam: Elsevier, 2009), 1143–49, doi:10.1016/B978-008045046-9.01907-0.

2. Albert Mehrabian and Norman Epstein, "A Measure of Emotional Empathy," *Journal of Personality* 40, no. 4 (Dec 1972): 525–43, doi:10.1111/j.1467-6494.1972.tb00078.x.

3. Mark H. Davis, "Measuring Individual Differences in Empathy: Evidence for a Multidimensional Approach," *Journal of Personality and Social Psychology* 44, no. 1 (1983): 113–26, doi:10.1037/0022-3514.44.1.113.

4. Meghan L. Healey and Murray Grossman, "Cognitive and Affective Perspective-Taking: Evidence for Shared and Dissociable Anatomical Substrates," *Frontiers in Neurology* 9, no. 491 (2018), doi:10.3389/fneur.2018.00491.

5. Lidewij W. Niezink et al., "Empathic Concern: Distinguishing between Tenderness and Sympathy," *Motivation and Emotion* 36, no. 4 (Dec 2012): 544–49, doi:10.1007/s11031-011-9276-z.

6. Davis, "Measuring Individual Differences in Empathy: Evidence for a Multidimensional Approach."

7. David F. Swink, "I Don't Feel Your Pain: Overcoming Roadblocks to Empathy," *Psychology Today*, March 7, 2013, https://www.psychologytoday.com/us/blog/threat-management/201303/i-dont-feel-your-pain-overcoming-roadblocks-empathy.

8. David Foster Wallace, "This is Water" (speech, Kenyon College, Gambier, OH, May 21, 2005).

9. Tania Singer, "The Neuronal Basis and Ontogeny of Empathy and Mind Reading: Review of Literature and Implications for Future Research," *Neuroscience & Biobehavioral Reviews* 30, no. 6 (2006): 855–63, doi:10.1016/j.neubiorev.2006.06.011.

10. Shalini Misra, "The iPhone Effect: The Quality of In-Person Social Interactions in the Presence of Mobile Devices," *Environment and Behavior* 48, no. 2 (2014): 275–98, doi:10.1177/0013916514539755.

11. Sara H. Konrath, Edward H. O'Brien, and Courtney Hsing, "Changes in Dispositional Empathy in American College Students Over Time: A Meta-Analysis," *Personality and Social Psychology Review* 15, no. 2 (2011): 180–98, doi:10.1177/1088868310377395.

12. Christopher Terry and Jeff Cain, "The Emerging Issue of Digital Empathy," *American Journal of Pharmaceutical Education* 80, no. 4 (May 2016), doi:10.5688/ajpe80458.

13. Tracy Alloway et al., "Is Facebook Linked to Selfishness? Investigating the Relationships among Social Media Use, Empathy, and Narcissism," *Social Networking* 3, no. 3 (Apr 2014): 150–58, doi:10.4236/sn.2014.33020.

14. Tobias Greitemeyer, Silvia Osswald, and Markus Brauer, "Playing Prosocial Video Games Increases Empathy and Decreases Schadenfreude," *Emotion* 10, no. 6 (2010): 796–802, doi:10.1037/a0020194.

15. Fernanda Herrera et al., "Building Long-Term Empathy: A Large-Scale Comparison of Traditional and Virtual Reality Perspective-Taking," *PLOS One* 13, no. 10, doi:10.1371/journal.pone.0204494.

16. "Macaques, Mirror Neurons, and the Power of Smiles," *Mindframe* (blog), August 17, 2012, http://mindframewithrobb.blogspot.com/2012/08/macaques-mirror-neurons-and-power-of.html.

17. V. S. Ramachandran, "Mirror Neurons and Imitation Learning as the Driving Force behind 'the Great Leap Forward' in Human Evolution," Edge.org, June 1, 2000, https://www.edge.org/3rd_culture/ramachandran/ramachandran_index.html.

18. L. Carr et al., "Neural Mechanisms of Empathy in Humans: A Relay from Neural Systems for Imitation to Limbic Areas," *Proceedings of the National Academy of Sciences* 100, no. 9 (Apr 2003), 5497–502, doi:10.1073/pnas.0935845100.

19. Dario Nardi, "Hormones, Sex and Personality Type," *Bulletin of Psychological Type* 26, no. 4 (2003), http://www.darionardi.com/BulletinArt9.html.

20. Jack van Honk et al., "Testosterone Administration Impairs Cognitive Empathy in Women Depending on Second-to-Fourth Digit Ratio," *Proceedings of the National Academy of Sciences* 108, no. 8 (Feb 2011), doi:10.1073/pnas.1011891108.

21. Nancy Eisenberg and Randy Lennon, "Sex Differences in Empathy and Related Capacities," *Psychological Bulletin* 94, no. 1 (1983): 100–31, doi:10.1037/0033-2909.94.1.100.

22. Rene Hurlemann, "Oxytocin Enhances Amygdala-Dependent, Socially Reinforced Learning and Emotional Empathy in Humans," *Journal of Neuroscience* 30, no. 14 (Apr 2010): 4999–5007, doi:10.1523/JNEUROSCI.5538-09.2010.

23. "People with Low Oxytocin Levels Suffer Reduced Empathy," Society for Endocrinology, November 7, 2016, https://www.endocrinology.org/press/press-releases/people-with-low-oxytocin-levels-suffer-reduced-empathy.

24. Mehrabian and Epstein, "A Measure of Emotional Empathy."

25. Mina Cikara, Emile G. Bruneau, and Rebecca R. Saxe, "Us and Them: Intergroup Failures of Empathy," *Current Directions in Psychological Science* 20, no. 3 (Nov 2017): 149–53, doi:10.1177/0963721411408713.

26. Richard L. Archer et al., "The Role of Dispositional Empathy and Social Evaluation in the Empathic Mediation of Helping," *Journal of Personality and Social Psychology* 40, no. 4 (1981), doi:10.1037/0022-3514.40.4.786.

27. Françoise Mathieu, "Running on Empty: Compassion Fatigue in Health Professionals," *Rehab & Community Care Medicine Magazine*, Spring 2007, http://www.compassionfatigue.org/pages/RunningOnEmpty.pdf.

28. Helen Riess, "The Science of Empathy," *Journal of Patient Experience* 4, no. 2 (June 2017): 74–77, doi:10.1177/2374373517699267.

29. Helen Riess, "Empathy Training for Resident Physicians: A Randomized Controlled Trial of a Neuroscience-Informed Curriculum," *Journal of General Internal Medicine* 27, no. 10 (Oct 2012): 1280–86, doi:10.1007/s11606-012-2063-z.

30. John D. Mayer and Glenn Geher, "Emotional Intelligence and the Identification of Emotion," *Intelligence* 22, no. 2 (Mar–Apr 1996): 89–113, doi:10.1016/S0160-2896(96)90011-2.

31. Roman Krznaric, "Can You Teach People to Have Empathy?" *BBC News*, June 29, 2015, https://www.bbc.com/news/magazine-33287727.

32. "Managing Mental Health Matters: Empathic Questions," Workplace Strategies for Mental Health, accessed February 4, 2020, https://www.workplacestrategiesformentalhealth.com/mmhm/pdf/articles/The_Power_of_Empathic_Questions.pdf.

33. Alison Wood Brooks and Leslie K. John, "The Surprising Power of Questions," *Harvard Business Review*, May–June 2018, https://hbr.org/2018/05/the-surprising-power-of-questions.

34. Arthur Aron et al., "The Experimental Generation of Interpersonal Closeness: A Procedure and Some Preliminary Findings," *Personality and Social Psychology Bulletin* 23, no. 4 (Apr 1997): 363–77, doi:10.1177/0146167297234003.

35. Daniel Jones, "The 36 Questions That Lead to Love," *New York Times*, January 9, 2015, https://www.nytimes.com/2015/01/11/style/36-questions-that-lead-to-love.html.

Chapter 11

1. Brooks and John, "The Surprising Power of Questions."

2. Alex Pentland, *Honest Signals: How They Shape Our World* (Cambridge, MA: MIT Press, 2010).

3. Baumgarten, "Curiosity as a Moral Virtue."

4. Feng and Magen, "Relationship Closeness Predicts Unsolicited Advice Giving in Supportive Interactions."

5. Aaron Ben-Zeev, "Will You Give Me Love in Return?" *Psychology Today*, October 10, 2008, https://www.psychologytoday.com/us/blog/in-the-name-love/200810/will-you-give-me-love-in-return.

6. Brooks and John, "The Surprising Power of Questions."

7. Yulia E. Chentsova-Dutton and Alexandra Vaughn, "Let Me Tell You What to Do: Cultural Differences in Advice-Giving," *Journal of Cross-Cultural Psychology* 43, no. 5 (2012): 687–703, doi:10.1177/0022022111402343.

8. Jolie Kerr, "How to Talk to People, According to Terry Gross," *New York Times, November 17, 2018,* https://www.nytimes.com/2018/11/17/style/self-care/terry-gross-conversation-advice.html.

9. Andrea L. Benin et al., "Qualitative Analysis of Mothers' Decision-Making about Vaccines for Infants: The Importance of Trust," *Pediatrics* 117, no. 5 (May 2006), 1532–41, doi:10.1542/peds.2005-1728.

10. Mazzocco et al., "This Story Is Not for Everyone: Transportability and Narrative Persuasion."

11. Jonathan R. Cohen, "Open-Minded Listening."

12. Todd B. Kashdan et al., "When Curiosity Breeds Intimacy: Taking Advantage of Intimacy Opportunities and Transforming Boring Conversations."

13. Brooks and John, "The Surprising Power of Questions."

14. Karen Huang, "It Doesn't Hurt to Ask: Question-Asking Increases Liking."

15. Christopher C. Gearhart and Graham D. Bodie, "Active-Empathic Listening as a General Social Skill: Evidence from Bivariate and Canonical Correlations," *Communication Reports* 24, no. 2 (2011): 86–98, doi:10.1080/08934215.2011.610731.

16. McKay and McKay, "How to Avoid Conversational Narcissism."

17. Tamir and Mitchell, "Disclosing Information about the Self Is Intrinsically Rewarding."

18. Brooks and John, "The Surprising Power of Questions."

19. Hal Gregersen, "Better Brainstorming," *Harvard Business Review*, March–April 2018, https://hbr.org/2018/03/better-brainstorming.

20. Robert T. Pate and Neville H. Bremer, "Guiding Learning through Skillful Questioning," *The Elementary School Journal* 67, no. 8 (May 1967): 417–22, doi:10.1086/460396.

21. Edgar H. Schein, *Humble Inquiry: The Gentle Art of Asking Instead of Telling* (San Francisco, Berrett-Koehler Publishers, 2013), 2.

22. "The Importance of Open-Ended Questions," Girls Empowerment Network, July 13, 2015, https://www.girlsempowermentnetwork.org/blog/the-importance-of-open-ended-questions.

23. Brett McKay and Kate McKay, "Social Briefing #8: How to Ask Open vs. Closed Questions," The Art of Manliness, May 25, 2017, https://www.artofmanliness.com/articles/social-briefing-8-better-conversations-asking-open-ended-questions.

24. Aron et al., "The Experimental Generation of Interpersonal Closeness: A Procedure and Some Preliminary Findings."

25. Susan Farrell, "Open-Ended vs. Closed-Ended Questions in User Research," Nielsen Norman Group, May 22, 2016, https://www.nngroup.com/articles/open-ended-questions.

26. David F. Swink, "I Don't Feel Your Pain: Overcoming Roadblocks to Empathy."

27. Nicholas Epley, "Be Mindwise: Perspective Taking vs. Perspective Getting," *The Psych Report*, April 16, 2014, http://thepsychreport.com/essays-discussion/be-mindwise-perspective-taking-vs-perspective-getting.

28. "Managing Mental Health Matters: Empathic Questions," Workplace Strategies for Mental Health.

Chapter 12

1. "Climate Change: How Do We Know?" Global Climate Change, updated January 28, 2020, https://climate.nasa.gov/evidence.

2. "Scientific Consensus: Earth's Climate is Warming," Global Climate Change, updated January 28, 2020, https://climate.nasa.gov/scientific-consensus.

3. Jan Dash and John Cook, "Global Warming & Climate Change Myths," Skeptical Science, accessed February 4, 2020, https://skepticalscience.com/argument.php.

4. Elizabeth Kolbert, "Why Facts Don't Change Our Minds," *New Yorker*, February 20, 2017, https://www.newyorker.com/magazine/2017/02/27/why-facts-dont-change-our-minds.

5. Julie Beck, "This Article Won't Change Your Mind," *Atlantic*, March 13, 2017, https://www.theatlantic.com/science/archive/2017/03/this-article-wont-change-your-mind/519093.

6. Melissa Denchak, "Are the Effects of Global Warming Really That Bad?" Natural Resources Defense Council, March 15, 2016, https://www.nrdc.org/stories/are-effects-global-warming-really-bad.

7. "New CDC Report Finds Extreme Summer Heat Kills More Than All Other Natural Disasters, Offers Help," SeniorJournal.com, June 7, 2013, http://seniorjournal.com/NEWS/Alerts/2013/20130607_New_CDC_Report.htm.

8. Rachael Post, "Personalising Climate Change through Open Data and Apps," *Guardian*, September 11, 2014, "https://www.theguardian.com/sustainable-business/2014/sep/11/climate-change-open-data-apps-government-environment-agency.

9. Heather Smith, "What's the Best Way to Communicate about Climate Change? This Expert Offers Some Insights," *Grist*, September 17, 2015, https://grist.org/climate-energy/whats-the-best-way-to-communicate-about-climate-change-this-expert-offers-some-insights.

10. Sabine Roeser, "Risk Communication, Public Engagement, and Climate Change: A Role for Emotions," *Risk Analysis* 32, no. 6 (Apr 2012): 1033–40, doi:10.1111/j.1539-6924.2012.01812.x.

11. "Human Brain," Basic Knowledge 101, accessed February 3, 2020, https://www.basicknowledge101.com/subjects/brain.html.

12. Mark D'Esposito and Bradley R. Postle, "The Cognitive Neuroscience of Working Memory," *Annual Review of Psychology* 66 (Jan 2015): 115–42, doi:10.1146/annurev-psych-010814-015031.

13. Alec T. Beall and Jessica L. Tracy, "Emotivational Psychology: How Distinct Emotions Facilitate Fundamental Motives," *Social and Personality Psychology Compass* 11, no. 2 (Feb 2017), doi:10.1111/spc3.12303.

14. Daniel Kahneman and Amos Tversky, "Prospect Theory: An Analysis of Decision under Risk," *Econometrica* 47, no. 2 (Mar 1979): 263–92, doi:10.2307/1914185.

15. Paul Slovic and Ellen Peters, "Risk Perception and Affect," *Current Directions in Psychological Science* 15, no. 6 (Dec 2006): 322–25, doi:10.1111/j.1467-8721.2006.00461.x.

16. "Backgrounder on Analysis of Cancer Risks in Populations Near Nuclear Facilities," United States Nuclear Regulatory Commission, updated May 28, 2019, https://www.nrc.gov/reading-rm/doc-collections/fact-sheets/bg-analys-cancer-risk-study.html.

17. Keith E. Stanovich and Richard F. West, "Individual Differences in Reasoning: Implications for the Rationality Debate?" *Behavioral and Brain Sciences* 23, no. 5 (2000): 645–65, doi:10.1017/S0140525X00003435.

18. Elizabeth A. Kensinger, "Remembering the Details: Effects of Emotion," *Emotion Review* 1, no. 2 (2009): 99–113, doi:10.1177/1754073908100432.

19. Emily Bobrow, "Fight Climate Change with Behavior Change," Behavioral Scientist, October 16, 2018, https://behavioralscientist.org/fight-climate-change-with-behavior-change.

20. Johns Hopkins Medical Institutions, "Why Emotionally Charged Events Are So Memorable," *Science Daily*, October 7, 2007, https://www.sciencedaily.com/releases/2007/10/071004121045.htm.

21. Lucas S. Broster, Lee X. Blonder, and Yang Jiang, "Does Emotional Memory Enhancement Assist the Memory-Impaired? *Frontiers in Aging Neuroscience* 4, no. 2 (2012), doi:10.3389/fnagi.2012.00002.

22. H. Kazui et al., "Impact of Emotion on Memory. Controlled Study of the Influence of Emotionally Charged Material on Declarative Memory in Alzheimer's Disease," British Journal of Psychiatry 177 (Oct 2000): 343–47, doi:10.1192/bjp.177.4.343.

23. Jag Bhalla, "The Cognitive Science of Kirk and Spock," Big Think, March 4, 2015, https://bigthink.com/errors-we-live-by/the-cognitive-science-of-kirk-and-spock.

24. Drake Baer, "How Only Being Able to Use Logic to Make Decisions Destroyed a Man's Life," *The Cut* (blog), *New York Magazine*, June 14, 2016, https://www.thecut.com/2016/06/how-only-using-logic-destroyed-a-man.html.

25. Antoine Bechara, "The Role of Emotion in Decision-Making: Evidence from Neurological Patients with Orbitofrontal Damage," *Brain and Cognition* 55, no. 1 (2004): 30–40, doi:10.1016/j.bandc.2003.04.001.

26. Jennifer S. Lerner et al., "Emotion and Decision Making," *Annual Review of Psychology* 66 (Jan 2015): 799–823, doi:10.1146/annurev-psych-010213-115043.

27. Shiri Cohen et al., "Eye of the Beholder: The Individual and Dyadic Contributions of Empathic Accuracy and Perceived Empathic Effort to Relationship Satisfaction," *Journal of Family Psychology* 26, no. 2 (2012): 236–45, doi:10.1037/a0027488.

28. Steven M. Graham et al., "The Positives of Negative Emotions: Willingness to Express Negative Emotions Promotes Relationships," *Personality and Social Psychology Bulletin* 34, no. 3 (Mar 2008): 394–406, doi:10.1177/0146167207311281.

29. Gerben A. van Kleef, Carsten K. W. De Dreu, and Antony S. R. Manstead, "The Interpersonal Effects of Anger and Happiness in Negotiations," *Journal of Personality and Social Psychology* 86, no. 1 (2004): 57–76, doi:10.1037/0022-3514.86.1.57.

30. Maarten J. J. Wubben, David DeCremer, and Eric van Dijk, "How Emotion Communication Guides Reciprocity: Establishing Cooperation through Disappointment and Anger," *Journal of Experimental Social Psychology* 45, no. 4 (July 2009): 987–90, doi:10.1016/j.jesp.2009.04.010.

31. Han Lin, William Tov, and Lin Qiu, "Emotional Disclosure on Social Networking Sites: The Role of Network Structure and Psychological Needs," *Computers in Human Behavior* 41 (2014): 342–50, doi:10.1016/j.chb.2014.09.045.

32. Peter Totterdell et al., "Evidence of Mood Linkage in Work Groups," *Journal of Personality and Social Psychology* 74, no. 6 (June 1998): 1504–15, doi:10.1037//0022-3514.74.6.1504.

33. Christopher K. Hsee et al., "The Effect of Power on Susceptibility to Emotional Contagion," *Cognition and Emotion* 4, no. 4 (1990): 327–40, doi:10.1080/02699939008408081.

34. Christian E. Waugh and Barbara L. Fredrickson, "Nice to Know You: Positive Emotions, Self–Other Overlap, and Complex Understanding in the Formation of a New Relationship," *Journal of Positive Psychology* 1, no. 2 (Apr 2006) 93–106, doi:10.1080/17439760500510569.

35. Arthur Aron, Elaine N. Aron, and Danny Smollan, "Inclusion of Other in the Self Scale and the Structure of Interpersonal Closeness," *Journal of Personality and Social Psychology* 63, no. 4 (1992): 596–612, doi:10.1037/0022-3514.63.4.596.

36. Lauri Nummenmaa et al., "Emotions Promote Social Interaction by Synchronizing Brain Activity across Individuals," Proceedings of the National Academy of Sciences 109, no. 24 (2012): 9599–604, doi:10.1073/pnas.1206095109.

37. N. Ambady et al., "Surgeons' Tone of Voice: A Clue to Malpractice History," *Surgery* 132, no. 1 (2002): 5–9, doi:10.1067/msy.2002.124733.

38. Benjamin J. Howard, "If You Can't Say Something Nice…" Neil Dymott Attorneys, accessed February 3, 2020, https://www.neildymott.com/if-you-cant-say-something-nice.

39. W. Levinson et al., "Physician-Patient Communication. The Relationship with Malpractice Claims among Primary Care Physicians and Surgeons," *Journal of the*

American Medical Association 277, no. 7 (Feb 1997): 553–59, doi:10.1001/jama.1997.03540310051034.

40. Renee Peltz Dennison, "Do Half of All Marriages Really End in Divorce?" *Psychology Today*, April 24, 2017, https://www.psychologytoday.com/us/blog/heart-the-matter/201704/do-half-all-marriages-really-end-in-divorce.

41. P. A. Andersen, Laura K. Guerrero, and Susanne M. Jones, "Nonverbal Behavior in Intimate Interactions and Intimate Relationships," *The SAGE Handbook of Nonverbal Communication* (Thousand Oaks, CA: SAGE Publications, 2006), 259–77.

Chapter 13

1. Paul Rozin and Edward B. Royzman, "Negativity Bias, Negativity Dominance, and Contagion," *Personality and Social Psychology Review* 5, no. 4 (Nov 2001): 296–320, doi:10.1207/S15327957PSPR0504_2.

2. Kendra Cherry, "What Is the Negativity Bias?" Verywell Mind, April 11, 2019, https://www.verywellmind.com/negative-bias-4589618.

3. Kennon M. Sheldon, Richard Ryan, and Harry T. Reis, "What Makes for a Good Day? Competence and Autonomy in the Day and in the Person," *Personality and Social Psychology Bulletin* 22, no. 12 (Dec 1996): 1270–79, doi:10.1177/01461672962212007.

4. Roy F. Baumeister et al., "Bad Is Stronger Than Good," *Review of General Psychology* 5, no. 4 (2001): 323–70, doi:10.1037//1089-2680.5.4.323.

5. Kyle Benson, "The Magic Relationship Ratio, According to Science," *The Gottman Relationship* (blog), The Gottman Institute, October 4, 2017, https://www.gottman.com/blog/the-magic-relationship-ratio-according-science.

6. Roy F. Baumeister and Brad Bushman, "Is Bad Stronger Than Good?" in *Social Psychology and Human Nature* (Boston: Cengage Learning, 2007), 373.

7. Rozin and Royzman, "Negativity Bias, Negativity Dominance, and Contagion."

8. Tiffany A. Ito et al., "Negative Information Weighs More Heavily on the Brain: The Negativity Bias in Evaluative Categorizations," *Journal of Personality and Social Psychology* 75, no. 4 (1998): 887–900, doi:10.1037/0022-3514.75.4.887.

9. Suzanne C. Segerstrom, "Optimism and Resources: Effects on Each Other and on Health over 10 Years," *Journal of Research in Personality* 41, no. 4 (2007): 772–86, doi:10.1016/j.jrp.2006.09.004.

10. Rozin and Royzman, "Negativity Bias, Negativity Dominance, and Contagion."

11. Henning Gibbons, Robert Schnuerch, and Jutta Stahl, "From Positivity to Negativity Bias: Ambiguity Affects the Neurophysiological Signatures of Feedback Processing," *Journal of Cognitive Neuroscience* 28, no. 4 (Jan 2016): 1–16, doi:10.1162/jocn_a_00921.

12. Rozin and Royzman, "Negativity Bias, Negativity Dominance, and Contagion."

13. Julie Haizlip et al., "Perspective: The Negativity Bias, Medical Education, and the Culture of Academic Medicine: Why Culture Change Is Hard," *Academic Medicine* 87, no. 9 (Sep 2012): 1205–9, doi:10.1097/ACM.0b013e3182628f03.

14. Joseph N. McDonald, "We're Not Happy Unless We're Unhappy: Conquering Negativity in the Workplace to Repair Company Culture and Increase Profitability," July 25, 2014, https://www.academia.edu/13222212/Were_Not_Happy_Unless_Were_Unhappy_Conquering_Negativity_in_the_Workplace_to_Repair_Company_Culture_and_Increase_Profitability.

15. Carolyn Doty, "The Relationship between Attention and the Negativity Bias in Memory," *Yale Review of Undergraduate Research in Psychology*, May 5, 2018, https://cpb-us-w2.wpmucdn.com/campuspress.yale.edu/dist/a/1215/files/2018/05/Attention-and-the-Negativity-Bias-in-Memory-Formatted-27e1fu8.pdf.

16. Maria Elizabeth Grabe and Rasha Kamhawi, "Hard Wired for Negative News? Gender Differences in Processing Broadcast News," *Communication Research* 33, no. 5 (Oct 2006): 346–69, doi:10.1177/0093650206291479.

17. Jackie K. Gollan et al., "Neural Substrates of Negativity Bias in Women With and Without Major Depression," *Biological Psychology* 109 (July 2015): 184–91, doi:10.1016/j.biopsycho.2015.06.003.

18. Mara Mather et al., "Amygdala Responses to Emotionally Valenced Stimuli in Older and Younger Adults," *Psychological Science* 15, no. 4 (2004): 259–63, doi:10.1111/j.0956-7976.2004.00662.x.

19. Michael A. Kisley, Stacey Wood, and Christina L. Burrows, "Looking at the Sunny Side of Life: Age-Related Change in an Event-Related Potential Measure of the Negativity Bias," *Psychological Science* 18, no. 9 (2007): 838–43, doi:10.1111/j.1467-9280.2007.01988.x.

20. Elisha Goldstein, "If You Can Name It, You Can Tame It," *Mindfulness & Psychotherapy*, Psych Central, updated January 6, 2014, https://blogs.psychcentral.com/mindfulness/2014/01/if-you-can-name-it-you-can-tame-it.

21. Benson, "The Magic Relationship Ratio, According to Science."

22. Fish, Rothermich, and Pell, "The Sound of (In)Sincerity."

23. Baumgarten, "Curiosity as a Moral Virtue."

24. Glaser, "Conversational Blind Spots."

25. Couture, "Giving Advice on Advice-Giving: A Conversation Analysis of Karl Tomm's Practice."

26. Lewicki, Polin, and Lount, "An Exploration of the Structure of Effective Apologies."

27. Robinson et al., "Actual Versus Assumed Differences in Construal: 'Naive Realism' in Intergroup Perception and Conflict."

Chapter 14

1. "Understanding the Stress Response," *Harvard Health Publishing*.

2. Diane Musho Hamilton, "Calming Your Brain During Conflict," *Harvard Business Review*, December 22, 2015, https://hbr.org/2015/12/calming-your-brain-during-conflict.

3. Kaufman, "The Pressing Need for Everyone to Quiet Their Egos."

4. van Rooyen, Durrheim, and Lindegger, "Advice-Giving Difficulties in Voluntary Counselling and Testing: A Distinctly Moral Activity."

5. Gearhart and Bodie, "Active-Empathic Listening as a General Social Skill: Evidence from Bivariate and Canonical Correlations."

6. Weger, Castle, and Emmett, "Active Listening in Peer Interviews: The Influence of Message Paraphrasing on Perceptions of Listening Skill."

7. Bavelas, Coates, and Johnson, "Listeners as Co-narrators."

8. David McNaughton et al., "Learning to Listen: Teaching an Active Listening Strategy to Preservice Education Professionals."

9. Rogers and Farson, *Active Listening.*

10. Brooks and John, "The Surprising Power of Questions."

11. DeVito, *The Interpersonal Communication Book,* 15th ed.

12. Robinson et al., "Actual Versus Assumed Differences in Construal: 'Naive Realism' in Intergroup Perception and Conflict."

13. "U.S. Divorce Rates and Statistics," DivorceSource.com, accessed February 4, 2020, https://www.divorcesource.com/ds/main/u-s-divorce-rates-and-statistics-1037.shtml.

14. "Marriage & Divorce," *American Psychological Association*, accessed February 4, 2020, https://www.apa.org/topics/divorce.

15. James L. Peterson and Nicholas Zill, "Marital Disruption, Parent-Child Relationships, and Behavior Problems in Children," *Journal of Marriage and Family* 48, no. 2 (May 1986): 295–307, doi:10.2307/352397.

16. "The Top 20 Family Arguments Revealed," Supanet.net, November 17, 2009, https://www.supanet.com/the-top-20-family-arguments-revealed-a5620.html.

17. "America's Most & Least Amicable Couples," Mattress Clarity, accessed February 4, 2020, https://www.mattressclarity.com/Infographics/amicable-couples.

18. Nicholas Zill, "What Couples with Children Argue About Most," *Institute for Family Studies* (blog), February 16, 2016, https://ifstudies.org/blog/what-couples-with-children-argue-about-most.

19. Diane Harris, "Poll: How Husbands and Wives Really Feel About Their Finances," *Money*, June 1, 2014, https://money.com/love-money-by-the-numbers.

20. "Kindergarten Class of 1998-99 (ECLS-K)," National Center for Education Statistics, accessed February 5, 2020, https://nces.ed.gov/ecls/kindergarten.asp.

21. Kahan et al., "'They Saw a Protest': Cognitive Illiberalism and the Speech-Conduct Distinction."

22. Michael W. Kraus and Dacher Keltner, "Social Class Rank, Essentialism, and Punitive Judgment," *Journal of Personality and Social Psychology* 105, no. 2 (2013): 247–61, doi:10.1037/a0032895.

23. Robinson et al., "Actual Versus Assumed Differences in Construal: 'Naive Realism' in Intergroup Perception and Conflict."

24. Brian D. Doss, Lorelei E. Simpson, and Andrew Christensen, "Why Do Couples Seek Marital Therapy?" *Professional Psychology: Research and Practice* 35, no. 6 (2004): 608–14, doi:10.1037/0735-7028.35.6.608.

25. Justin A. Lavner, Benjamin R. Karney, and Thomas N. Bradbury, "Does Couples' Communication Predict Marital Satisfaction, or Does Marital Satisfaction Predict Communication?" *Journal of Marriage and Family* 78, no. 3 (2016): 680–94, doi:10.1111/jomf.12301.

26. M. D. Johnson et al., "Problem-Solving Skills and Affective Expressions as Predictors of Change in Marital Satisfaction," *Journal of Consulting and Clinical Psychology* 73, no. 1 (Feb 2005): 15–27, doi:10.1037/0022-006X.73.1.15.

27. Tamir and Mitchell, "Disclosing Information about the Self Is Intrinsically Rewarding."

Index

apologies, 80–81, 181, 188

Aron, Arthur, 138, 150

Ask Pivot, 147–149, 193–194

attention

    audience, 42–43

    extroversion and, 65

    introversion and, 67

    listening and, 46

    relationships and, 120–121

attitude

    listening, 120–121

    money, 191

audience attention, 42–43

authenticity

    engagement and, 175

    questions and, 96

    sincerity vs., 77–78

awareness

    advice and, 103

    empathy and, 136

    meditation and, 22

    self-, 9, 22, 103

B

Barker, Joel A., 196

"battle of agendas," 59, 92

Baumeister, Roy, 175

bias. See negativity bias

Blockbuster (video rental), 56

blood pressure, 19, 107

body language, 46, 78, 121, 153, 167–168, 180

Brain Rules (Medina), 18, 164

Brooks, Alison Wood, 142–143

Bursky, Edward C., 79

C

Cain, Susan, 62, 64, 69

Carlin, George, 106

Carnegie, Dale, 123

cell phones, 20–21, 41–43

Center for Mindful Self-Compassion, 33

Charan, Ram, 117

children, curiosity in, 53–54

Chodron, Pema, 50

Cialdini, Robert, 48

climate change, 158–159, 161

communication. See also conversation

    curiosity and, 53

    digital, 88

    gender and, 163–164

    neuroscience of, 90–92

    as portion of daily activity, 88

    rejection and, 92

    relationships and, 193

    story and, 93–95

compassion, 19–20

confidence

    authenticity and, 78

    extroversion and, 71, 73

    listening and, 121

    self-help industry and, 31–32

    success and, 9

conflict

    apologies and, 81

    brain chemistry in, 186

    empathy and, 136

    hacks, 187–189

    listening and, 120, 136, 187

    money and, 191–192

    positivity and, 179

Google, 55

Gottman, John, 179–180

Grant, Adam, 69

gratitude, 20, 22–23, 112, 166, 182

Gregerson, Hal, 149

Groopman, Jerome, 119

Gross, Terry, 44–45

H

hacks

    conflict, 187–189

    empathy, 136–137

    happiness, 16–17

    health, 18–19

    negativity, 178–179

Hamilton, Diane, 186

Hanson, Rick, 172

happiness, 9

    activities for, 16–17

    control over, 14–15

    curiosity and, 57

    diet and, 19

    exercise and, 18

    genetics and, 15–16

    hacks, 16–17

    relationships and, 23–24

    variance in, 14

Harvard Business Review, 21, 79, 117, 142–143

Hay, Louise, 32

health

    curiosity and, 56–57

    diet and, 19

    gratitude and, 22

    hacks, 18–19

    kindness and, 20

meditation and, 22

    relationships and, 23–24

heart disease, 18–19

Heibeck, Tracy, 143

helping others, 19–20

Herrera, Fernanda, 130

heuristics, 29–30

"high activity," 144

Hoffeld, David, 47, 168

Honest Signals: How They Shape Our World (Pentland and Heibeck), 143

honesty

    questions and, 52

    sincerity and, 76

hormones, 34–35, 93, 132–133, 148. *See also* adrenaline; oxytocin

How Doctors Think (Groopman), 119

How of Happiness, The: A Scientific Approach to Getting the Life You Want (Lyubomirsky), 14

How to Win Friends and Influence People (Carnegie), 123

I

Influential Mind, The (Sharot), 166–167

interrupting, 46, 116, 122, 136, 165, 180, 187

introversion

    acetylcholine and, 67

    in core of personality, 64–65

    description of, 68

    and eliciting of information, 72

    extroversion *vs.,* 65–66

    friendships and, 66

    genetics and, 67

    leadership and, 70

    listening and, 72

relationships and, 66, 71, 73

risk-taking and, 66

J

Jobs, Steve, 70

John, Leslie K., 142–143

K

Kahneman, Daniel, 15

Kashdan, Todd, 15–16, 57, 59

Kassem, Suzy, 184

Kerr, Jolie, 44–45

kindness, 19–20

Kodak, 55

Krznarichas, Roman, 136

L

Larson, Vicki, 189

leadership

    curiosity and, 53

    extroversion and, 65

    extroverts *vs.* introverts in, 70

    introverts and, 66

    listening and, 117

    sincerity and, 79

Leiserowitz, Anthony, 159

Levenson, Robert, 179–180

listening

    active, 46–48, 117–123

    Active-Empathic Listening Scale, 121

    advice and, 121, 136

    agendas and, 2, 119, 188

    attitude, 120–121

confidence and, 121

conflict and, 120, 136, 187

conversation and, 116

demonstrating, 123

engagement and, 40–41, 45–48

intent, 123

interrupting and, 122

introversion and, 72

passive, 117–118

pausing and, 122–123

persuasion and, 110–112

radical, 136

relationships and, 119–120

selective, 118–119

skills, 117–118

trust and, 118, 120, 187

Loewenstein, George, 52

"low consistency," 144

Lyubomirsky, Sonja, 12

M

Making Time (Taylor), 54

Manson, Mark, 28

marriage. *See* relationships

Medina, John, 18, 164

meditation, 21–22

"meformers," 89

Mehrabian, Albert, 133

memory

    conflict and, 186

    emotion and, 161

    exercise and, 18

    negativity bias and, 177

Mencken, H. L., 26

minds, wandering, 42

mirror neurons, 130–131

Mitchell, Jason P., 90

mobile devices, 20–21. *See also* smartphones

Money Magazine, 190

Myers-Briggs Type Indicator, 65

N

"naïve realism," 106, 108, 191

negativity bias

    defined, 174

    emotions and, 177

    as hard-wired, 175–176

    negative potential and, 176–177

    questions and, 175

negativity hacks, 178–179

Netflix, 56

neurotransmitters, 34–35, 67. *See also* acetylcholine; dopamine

New I do, The: Reshaping Marriage for Skeptics, Realists and Rebels (Larson and Gadoua), 189

New York Times, 44–45

nonverbal communication, 46, 78, 121, 153, 167–168, 180

Novella, Steven, 28

O

oxytocin, 33–35, 89, 91, 94, 109, 133

P

Pentland, Alex, 143

personality. *See* extroversion; introversion

perspective-taking, empathic concern *vs.,* 128, 152–153

persuasion

    advice and, 105–108

    listening and, 110–112

    logic and, 108

    "rule of consistency" and, 108

    stress and, 3, 107–108

    "transportability" and, 106

phones, 20–21, 41–43

positive thinking, 9, 30–31, 178

Power of Curiosity, The (Kashdan), 57

prejudice, 29

Pursuit of Attention, The (Derber), 92

Q

questions. *See also* communication

    about Ask Pivot, 202–204

    advice *vs.,* 104

    agenda-laden, 145–146

    Ask Pivot, 147–148

    conflict and, 181, 187–189

    curiosity and, 146

    empathy and, 137–138, 151–153

    for engagement, 44–45, 47–48

    engagement and, 44–45, 47–48, 144

    follow-up, 47–48, 96, 137, 148–149

    full-switch, 148

    introductory, 147

    lack of, 142–144

    negativity bias and, 175

    open, 149–151

    sincerity and, 76–77, 83

CPSIA information can be obtained
at www.ICGtesting.com
Printed in the USA
LVHW091730040222
709849LV00003B/4/J

9 780974 876320